To Carole
Thanks
You rock! E

MW01222574

THE VISIBLE SUBCONSCIOUS

Let your inner magic
come alive!

THE VISIBLE SUBCONSCIOUS

DISCOVER THE ART OF PARTNERING WITH
YOUR SUBCONSCIOUS, UNLOCK HIDDEN
POTENTIALS FOR PERSONAL
TRANSFORMATION

PONZ MANANTAN

Solid
Echo
PRESS

www.unsealedminds.com

First Edition 2024

ISBN: 979-8-9869655-0-5 (paperback)

ISBN: 979-8-9869655-1-2 (digital)

To my incredible parents, whose unwavering support has fueled the pursuit of our dreams.
To my dear siblings, Sheila, Chris, Drew, and Kyla Dee, each a unique ray of light in the tapestry of life.
To my friends and research participants, whose open-mindedness and unwavering belief in me propelled me forward on this odyssey of exploring life's boundless possibilities. Your presence has been instrumental in making previously unseen aspects of existence visible.
To my subconscious mind, which continues to amaze me now more than ever.
And to Almighty God, the Master Artist of Life and Creation. Thank you all for being the guiding stars throughout this remarkable endeavor.

CONTENTS

INTRODUCTION

Brace yourself for a mind-bending exploration of the human mind, where the invisible becomes visible, revealing a part that holds the master key to unlocking the mind's true potential. In this book, we embark on an awe-inspiring journey into the world of the visible subconscious mind, where extraordinary possibilities await those brave enough to delve into the depths of their own psyche. Get ready to challenge your perceptions and join me on a transformational journey unlike any other.

Scholars have been captivated by the human mind for centuries, considering it a complex and intriguing entity. Thanks to advancements in neuroscience and psychology, we have gained deeper insights into its workings, including both the conscious and subconscious aspects. However, despite extensive research and exploration, much remains to be uncovered, particularly concerning the subconscious mind, which still shrouds many of its workings in mystery.

Many often regard the subconscious mind as a hidden and intangible entity, beyond our immediate control, and challenging to access. It is believed to store our deepest fears, desires, and memories, playing a critical role in shaping our thoughts, emotions, and behaviors.

While the conscious mind is commonly perceived as dominant, it is important to note that the subconscious exerts considerable influence on our day-to-day lives. In fact, Young (2018) stated in the magazine *New Scientist* that about 95% of brain activity is unconscious.[1]

Consider the following example which underscores the distinction between the functions of our conscious and unconscious minds. According to Mlodinow (2012), conscious thought proves invaluable for tasks such as engineering or understanding mathematical equations. It is the rapid and instinctive responses of the unconscious that becomes paramount for protecting us from immediate dangers, in scenarios like dodging snake bites, maneuvering through unexpected road hazards, or identifying potential threats from others.[2]

In a 2021 blog post by Brian Tracy, the author discussed how the subconscious mind, sometimes referred to as the unconscious mind, plays a significant role in storing each individual's experiences.[3]

From my experience in the Information Technology Industry, I like to compare the subconscious mind to a storage unit filled with countless programs. Each program comprises a set of instructions executed in specific situations, similar to automatic responses or mental shortcuts. These mental habits significantly influence our actions and emotions. For every object encountered or situation faced, there's a program dictating our thoughts, feelings, and actions. The coordination is so swift that we often react to stimuli before consciously realizing it. Think of inadvertently walking face-first into a spider web and doing the awkward panic dance.

Consider the multitude of habits and programs we form and accumulate over the years. Whether these habits are positive or negative, the subconscious mind runs these programs automatically, sometimes causing us to repeat actions despite our conscious efforts to stop. Relying solely on willpower may not be enough to change these ingrained habits.

Have you encountered individuals who've experimented with techniques such as creating vision boards, reciting daily affirmations, or repeating goal statements in front of a mirror? While these methods aim to engage the subconscious mind, the number of successful outcomes might pale in comparison to those who tried and abandoned the practice. That's when New Year's resolutions are born each year, and, like a phoenix rising from the ashes, appearing much the same the following year.

Why is it important to access the subconscious mind? Because it's at this level where we can effectively alter deeply ingrained programs, particularly the unpleasant ones. By making changes or eliminating outdated patterns, we create space for new, and hopefully more beneficial, ones to emerge. However, the challenge lies in consciously accessing and reshaping these subconscious patterns. It is also at this level that we uncover profound insights, reveal hidden wisdom, and tap into latent talents. The author vividly recalls an intriguing account involving his colleague in the shower. One day, while showering, the colleague abruptly turned off the water and began urgently calling out his wife's name. Alarmed, she rushed to his side, fearing the worst, only to find him excitedly explaining a breakthrough in a computer programming code that had eluded him for days—an idea that had struck him while showering!

The subconscious mind functions like a robust figure handling all the heavy lifting in the mind's background, yet its voice is soft. When individuals pose questions, seek wisdom, or yearn for insights, most struggle to hear its whispers. And when least expected, the answers often surface during mundane tasks like washing dishes, driving, showering, or even dreaming. These eureka moments are instances when that faint voice imparts sought-after revelations. Alternatively, people carve out moments of mental tranquility to listen to their subconscious, be it through meditation, relaxation, or downtime.

But what if there was a method to unlock the full potential of our subconscious minds, enabling us to directly see and engage with it, and leverage its power to transform our lives? This is the premise of the book you are about to read: a journey into the unknown realm of the visible subconscious.

The primary purpose of *The Visible Subconscious: Meet Yours* is to present readers with a new and effective approach to contacting the subconscious mind and unlocking its power. It is a force that influences the thoughts and actions, a trusted ally that can be fearless.

By making the subconscious visible, individuals can attain a deeper understanding of themselves, their motivations, and the underlying patterns shaping their thoughts and behaviors. This empowers them to change some of these deep-seated programs. How? By literally witnessing a visible and interactive manifestation of their subconscious mind and seeking its assistance!

The concept of a visible subconscious has become increasingly relevant in our modern world, where there is a growing emphasis on personal growth and self-discovery. As interest in topics such as mental well-being, mindfulness, and unlocking human potential continues to rise, many individuals are actively seeking ways to access the depths of their subconscious minds. The visible subconscious can be likened to your subconscious mind on steroids!

This book explores the groundbreaking idea that we can perceive and interact with the subconscious mind, utilizing it readily like the conscious mind. Through stories of real individuals who have awakened their ability to engage with their visible subconscious minds, this book demonstrates the possibilities of tapping into this powerful tool to transform one's life. From altering emotions and beliefs to improving relationships and overcoming anxieties, the visible subconscious can serve as a formidable instrument in realizing our biggest aspirations.

The Visible Subconscious: Meet Yours is not a primer on hypnosis, nor does it dissect the subconscious mind. Instead, it comprises a collection of transcribed sessions, experiences, and insights from individuals who have harnessed the power of the visible subconscious to enhance their lives in profound and unexpected ways.

Catering to a diverse readership, ranging from novices with minimal knowledge of hypnosis and the subconscious mind to seasoned practitioners seeking deeper insights, this book offers something valuable for everyone.

For newcomers, it serves as an accessible gateway, demystifying select areas in the world of hypnosis and providing a profound introduction to the subconscious. It lays the groundwork for comprehending these concepts and their potential positive impacts on life.

Seasoned practitioners will find an illuminating exploration of a new technique for engaging with the subconscious, accompanied by real-life narratives to enrich their expertise.

Regardless of your prior knowledge, this book promises to bolster your understanding and inspire you to unlock the latent potential of your mind. For those seeking additional information and resources, the author's website, www.unsealedminds.com/visible-subconscious, serves as a valuable resource hub.

The author structured the book into several chapters, each touching on different facets of the visible subconscious. The initial chapter sets the stage by exploring the reality of hypnosis, leading to the discovery of the visible subconscious. Subsequent chapters unravel the journey of various individuals as they acquire this ability and utilize their visible subconscious to enhance diverse aspects of their lives, including relationships, careers, and personal growth.

Chapter Five discusses the testing conducted to verify the visible subconscious' influence over the body. In Chapter Eight, readers encounter a brief interview with this remarkable form, unveiling the extent of its capabilities and the secret to making it work effectively.

The concluding chapter presents various scenarios where individuals employed their visible subconscious forms to tackle diverse challenges. Towards the book's end, readers will find a short quiz designed to help them discover if they can be hypnotized. The author also included exercises that readers can do themselves, which may help them unleash their own personal visible subconscious.

Consider Matt's experience as an exemplary case. Following his COVID-19 booster shot, he encountered various side-effects, including headache, fever, fatigue, and pain at the injection site. Calling upon his visible subconscious to appear before him, Matt sought assistance in alleviating the vaccine's side-effects. Almost immediately, he observed a reduction in his headache by about 90%. The sensation of warmth on the injected area preceding the dissipation of pain surprised him. Additionally, he utilized his visible subconscious to facilitate healthier dietary choices.

In Laura's narrative, her visible subconscious acted as a catalyst for embracing positive thinking. By redirecting her subconscious focus from negativity to positivity, she not only experienced feeling happier but also witnessed improvements in her marital relationship. This shift resembled rewiring her brain for a sunnier perspective, and the results speak for themselves!

The author introduces an innovative approach to establish a productive bond with the subconscious mind, as depicted in the stories. By adhering to a set of simple yet effective communication strategies, individuals can rapidly rewire their brains via the visible subconscious. These techniques serve as the core secrets to making the visible subconscious successfully work for a person.

Imagine having the ability to see and interact with your own visible subconscious. What would you choose to improve about yourself? What would be the first goal you'd seek its help with?

This new concept is the author's initial contribution to helping people in their quest to better themselves. In a world that seems to be even more chaotic each day, may this be a light that illuminates your path as you navigate the wilderness of life. The author also hopes to inspire others to freely share their own light, assisting many in discovering theirs.

Throughout the book, individuals' names have been changed to safeguard their privacy. The term "visub" is recurrently used as a shorthand for the "visible subconscious."

In conversational exchanges, online slang such as 'laugh out loud' (LOL) is frequently employed to convey humor. In these instances, LOL (or lol) has been used accordingly.

As you set off on this adventure, I invite you to temporarily set aside what you already know. Prepare to be challenged, inspired, and enlightened. Each chapter holds the promise of unveiling fresh insights into the mind's capabilities and its profound influence. So go ahead, turn the page, and let's embark on this incredible journey of discovering an elevated level of self-improvement!

1

UNVEILING HYPNOSIS AND THE VISIBLE SUBCONSCIOUS

 "The mind that opens up to a new idea never returns to its original size."

— ALBERT EINSTEIN

Many individuals are likely familiar with the concept of hypnosis. They may have encountered it through reading, hearing about others' experiences, or even witnessing hypnosis shows in person or online. However, for those who have not undergone it, their reactions can vary from awe and fascination to confusion and skepticism. Some may even quickly dismiss what they have witnessed as staged performances.

According to Michael Yapko (2012, p. 7), "hypnosis is a process of focused attention, heightened suggestibility, and deep relaxation."[1] This heightened state of subconscious awareness opens the door to accessing and changing certain beliefs and habits (or "programs") that reside within the subconscious.

Stage hypnotists often craft the illusion of absolute control, giving the impression that they can command individuals to do anything they say. This dramatic flair undoubtedly enhances the entertainment aspect of the performance. However, it's crucial to recognize that participants retain awareness of their surroundings and are unlikely to act against their own beliefs or values. This constraint also applies to clinical hypnosis, where the effectiveness primarily relies on suggestion and the willingness of participants to engage in the process.

In this chapter, we explore Matt's first-hand experience of the realities of hypnosis. Matt, a middle-aged married man, embarks on a remarkable exploration that leads to the astounding discovery of his visible subconscious (visub).

During one of our conversations, I asked Matt about his thoughts on hypnosis. He admitted he wasn't sure, but seemed open to giving it a shot to find out its authenticity. One aspect that really caught his attention was past life regression. He'd heard stories of people going back in time, describing past lives with unique identities and in places they'd never visited before. What made it even more fascinating for him was when some details they mentioned about these places turned out to be surprisingly accurate in the real world.

Past life regression involves guiding individuals into a relaxed state where they can access and explore past life memories or experiences. While some may dismiss this as mere hallucinations, there are instances where past lives seem connected to current behavioral issues or beliefs, prompting consideration of its potential validity. Weiss (2012), a traditional psychotherapist, recounts his experiences using past life regression during hypnotherapy sessions with patients in his book *Many Lives Many Masters*.[2] Initially, a patient under his care showed no improvements, but after conducting a past life regression, significant improvement was observed. This approach helps patients uncover and address unresolved issues from past lives, facilitating emotional healing and personal improvement.

Given Matt's Information Technology background which highlights his logical and analytical nature, I prepared myself with techniques designed to bypass his logical mind and access his subconscious.

We agreed to meet again two weeks later. On the appointed day, we convened in my office, a modest space on the top floor of an old three-story brick building. I invited Matt to settle into the reclining sofa while I closed the two sash windows and drew the curtains. Despite it being the middle of summer in 2021, a remnant of the previous Christmas—a white-and-red snowman stocking—still hung between the windows. I had closed the office the previous year due to the COVID-19 pandemic.

I was pleasantly surprised by how quickly Matt relaxed and entered a deep state of hypnosis during the induction process. Guiding him along, I led him down a hallway lined with numerous doors on either side. I instructed him that upon reaching the door at the end and stepping into the light beyond, he would find himself immersed in one of his past lives, which he would then describe to me. The following transcript encapsulates the essence of that session:

> **Matt:** I'm standing on the street, surrounded by cobblestones. I see buildings around me that have white exteriors with exposed wooden frames. There are houses and shops lining both sides of the street.
> **PM:** Can you see any landmarks or notable features?
> **Matt:** It looks like an old street. The houses look like cakes, larger on top and smaller at the bottom. I see a

brick bridge spanning the upper levels. There are carts and people around.

PM: Take a moment to examine yourself. What do you see?

Matt: I'm standing on some cobbles. I notice I'm wearing cracked shoes and a white apron over my pants.

PM: Any other details about your appearance?

Matt: I look dirty. My shoes are old, and the apron is grubby.

PM: What made your clothes dirty?

Matt: I was making something. I think it was leather belts! And I've got polish on my hands.

PM: Can you determine the time period?

Matt: It feels old—maybe the 1700s. But I'm not sure.

PM: Describe your surroundings and occupation in more detail.

Matt: I see a shop with belts hanging from the roof. I have a thick wooden table, and I have tools to make little holes. My main tool is a hammer, and I can hit the top of the tool to make a hole in the leather to make a belt. I have a mustache and black hair.

PM: Is this what you do for a living?

Matt: Yes. I make belts, and I think I repair shoes.

PM: What country do you think you're in?

Matt: I'm in England. Maybe in York. It's not a big place.

PM: Do you have a family?

Matt: I have a daughter, Jenny, and she runs downstairs into the store from upstairs. She is six, has long hair, and helps out. And I have a wife named Jennifer. Her hair is up, and she is cooking soup. We live upstairs in the store.

I like to go to the pub and have lunch. My friend works there. I can get a beer and some bread, and talk to him.

PM: What's your name?

Matt: Mark.

PM: Do you possess any particular talents or skills in this lifetime?

Matt: I can put designs. I create my own intricate designs on the belts. I draw them on paper and then burn them into the leather using specialized stamps which I have to pay for. I can fish.

PM: What else?

Matt: I sometimes like to sing from time to time, usually with friends at the pub. But I don't think I'm any good at it.

PM: Any favorite songs you enjoy singing?

Matt: We tend to sing whatever strikes our fancy at the pub.

PM: Is there anyone else in your lifetime besides your family?

Matt: I just have my friends and my family. My parents have passed away. My wife is just in the house, she sews.

PM: Okay, Mark, let's transition to your time of death. On the count of three, describe what's happening. One, two, three.

Matt: ...I am feeling terribly sick—old and frail. My wife is here.

PM: How old are you at this time?

Matt: In my sixties.

PM: And what illness are you battling?

Matt: Pneumonia.

We delved further into the moments when he transcended his physical form, immersing ourselves in the vivid imagery of his journey. He painted a picture of finding himself in an obscure realm, shrouded in darkness, with no discernible sights to guide him. Yet, amidst the void, he described a gradual progression towards a luminous source, which he portrayed as radiant and infused with an overwhelming sense of tranquility.

Transitioning to the period when he was preparing for his subsequent incarnation, he recounted a surreal encounter with a dark focal point, seemingly in motion on the other side. Driven by curiosity, he felt compelled to explore further, perceiving it as a pathway that traversed the point and guided him towards his destination.

Realizing that we had only scratched the surface of the intriguing facets of hypnosis, I suggested delving even deeper into another captivating journey stored within his subconscious mind—a significant past life. Encouraging his subconscious to lead the way, I urged him to revisit a pivotal lifetime. Below is the continuation of the transcribed session:

> **Matt:** I'm wearing an armor, and my helmet has a distinctive metal ridge. I think I'm in France. I recognize the suit. It's heavy and there's fabric under the plate on my shoulder. My sword rests on a bench nearby. There are other soldiers around, all in armor like me. We're in an old castle, and the room we're in is adorned with moldings on the walls like cake. In the armory, there are swords, shields, and other decorations. Above the door hangs a large flag that resembles a royal crest. The doors are huge, heavy, and made of wood. The doors are massive, constructed of sturdy wood with metal bolts. They're open, and we're heading through into another room where the horses are kept. There's a lot of people here.
> I have all my gear, including a long, heavy, and incredibly sharp sword. I notice people riding out on horses, and I realize I'm waiting for one, too. It seems we're preparing to go out to the front of the castle. There's a

larger man here, wearing blue clothes and a white apron. He's directing people and assigning horses. It's loud and many people are shouting.

A horse is brought to me, and I climb onto a stool with the help of two others to steady myself due to the weight of the armor. I struggle to get my foot into the stirrup, but some boys assist me in mounting the horse. Once on, I grasp the reins, and we begin to move.

We pass through a large square door, and I can see the path ahead crowded with people. We eventually make it out to the front. From the castle, I can see a vast field leading up to the castle wall, and beyond that, a river. As we ride onto the grass, we begin organizing into lines.

PM: What's happening?

Matt: I don't know. We're getting into formation. There are two bridges over the river.

PM: Do you recognize the river?

Matt: No, I'm not familiar with it.

PM: Can you hear what people are saying?

Matt: People are conversing with each other. We're all waiting for someone to arrive on horseback.

PM: Do you know who that person is?

Matt: He's our leader, though I don't know what his name is. He's the one we follow.

PM: What language are they speaking in?

Matt: It's French. I can hear them talking now. I don't know what they're saying.

PM: Do you understand French?

Matt: (shaking his head) Uh-uh.

PM: How come?

Matt: I don't know; I can kind of hear what they're saying... I think people were asking... they're talking in French. I can't understand the words that they're saying, but I have a sense that they're discussing how long we'll be waiting.

PM: What's your purpose there?

Matt: We have to march out or ride out to another place. I'm not sure if we're going to fight or if we're accompanying him somewhere. There aren't enough of us to fight anything big.

I suggested to Matt to fast forward a day ahead.

Matt: We're camping on the road. One is sitting. I'm sitting around the fire. We've set up tents off the road. We're cooking rabbits. I'm getting hungry.

Once again, I suggested moving another day ahead.

Matt: We're riding through the countryside. We can't stay on the path because there's not much space. We're following in groups. I think we're reinforcements.
... there's fighting and we're going to help. We're positioned at the side. More people are coming.
... I'm on the ground. I have a sword within me, a sword! My sword is gone. I'm lying on the grass. My helmet's hurting my neck.

PM: Where are you?

Matt: I don't know. I'm lying in the field.

PM: Do you know what year it is?

Matt: 16... no. 1652? I'm not sure, 16...

PM: It's okay.

After bringing Matt out of the hypnotic state, I noticed a sense of astonishment in his expression. He eagerly shared his experience, describing how he could genuinely feel the weight of the armor as if it were draped over him, and the visuals he witnessed felt incredibly real.

Such positive feedback was encouraging, especially considering it was his first encounter with hypnosis.

The idea of past lives ignites debate, as our memories are typically anchored in experiences from our present existence that we can easily recall. However, the ability to remember events from past lives raises a profound question: are these recollections simply products of our imagination, or do they suggest that there are aspects of memory that transcend our current understanding? This could point to a deeper insight yet to be uncovered, especially since we can see evidence of past life recall but do not fully grasp the process behind how it works.

In the thought-provoking episode "Language of the Divine Matrix" from Gaia's television series *Missing Links*, renowned speaker Gregg Braden explores groundbreaking scientific revelations that challenge our traditional understanding of memory storage (Gaia, 2019).[3] Braden disputes the long-held belief that memories are stored solely in the brain's neurons. Instead, he suggests that neurons act more like sensitive biological antennas, tuning into a universal field—a cosmic database where memories are intricately stored.

This concept goes beyond theory. Engineers, inspired by nature, are moving past silicon chips and applying these insights to create next-generation computer technology. These revolutionary chips use a single droplet of highly structured water, compressed within the chip, to interface with computers. Researchers have found that entire libraries of information can be stored in that chip, sparking curiosity about where it all resides. Even more fascinating is their realization that the information isn't confined to the water itself—it's stored in a field connected to the droplet, extending beyond the chip and machine.

This discovery could profoundly change how we access and interact with information in our everyday lives, opening up exciting questions about the future of data storage. Just imagine the breakthroughs we might see in the next twenty years!

This unconventional perspective not only revolutionizes technology but also prompts us to reconsider how information—including thoughts and creations—exists in the world around us. Could this concept help explain the mysteries of past life regression? Some individuals claim to have lived as famous historical figures, such as Cleopatra, and it's not uncommon for multiple people to make the same assertion. This phenomenon evokes intriguing questions about the reliability and reality of these past life experiences.

Is it possible that these reports suggest a shared field of consciousness, where memories or archetypes of notable figures are more accessible? When people explore past lives, could they be tapping into a collective memory or frequency connected to these well-known personalities? Alternatively, could individuals access their own unique past lives by tuning into their personal frequency within this expansive field? These questions challenge our understanding of past lives and consciousness, hinting that memories and experiences may be part of a deeply interconnected web.

Nicola Tesla once said, "My brain is only a receiver, in the universe there is a core from which we obtain knowledge, strength, and inspiration. I have not penetrated into the secret of this core, but I know that it exists."

In *The Case For Reincarnation*, Danelek (2010) recounts documented instances where past life memories retrieved through hypnosis were substantiated by historical records. He also discusses accounts of children recalling intricate details of past lives, some of which were independently verified, offering compelling support for the phenomenon of reincarnation.[4]

AUGUST 2, 2021

Approximately a week after our meeting, Matt returned to the office, eager for another session.

During my time in Australia a few years ago, I had the opportunity to witness a mesmerizing hypnosis performance that featured an intriguing act. The hypnotist asked the volunteers to imagine watching a show on a large screen, and eventually, the characters would step out of the television and interact with them.

Inspired by this, I decided to experiment with a similar idea during one of Matt's sessions. Guiding him into a trance state, I provided the suggestion and keenly observed his eye movements and the noticeable facial expressions that unfolded as he embarked on a journey into his inner world. I asked Matt to describe what he was experiencing. Still with eyes closed and in a trance state, he shared that a female figure from the TV had stepped out of the screen. Curious, I asked what she was doing, and after a momentary pause, he said that she was rubbing against him. Although uncertain whether he was seeing a person or a feline companion, I chose not to go deeper into the specifics and gently brought him out of hypnosis. As he opened his eyes, he appeared momentarily lost in thought before expressing his awe at how vivid and real the encounter had felt. It was indeed a person he had seen, not a cat!

So far, Matt had experienced three distinct and realistic scenarios through hypnosis, heightening his anticipation of what lay ahead. I inquired if he had any personal concerns he wished to address. He claimed not to have any, so we agreed to explore another facet of the hypnotic realm. And back into hypnosis, he went.

Drawing upon another trick often used by stage hypnotists, I suggested that when someone tapped or touched the lower part of his arm, he would experience an increasing sense of excitement. To gauge the effectiveness of this suggestion, I brought Matt out of hypnosis and tapped his arm. There was no immediate reaction. I tapped it again. Eventually, he wore a sheepish smile. When asked, he compared the sensation to the excitement he felt during his teenage years when he had a crush on a girl at school. I tapped it a third time. The experience fascinated him.

To determine the duration of this suggestion's impact, I left it with him, bidding him farewell for the day while maintaining contact. On the third day after our session, Matt reported that the feeling still surfaced but had diminished in intensity. By the fifth day, it had vanished entirely, and tapping his arm elicited no response. The suggestion's effect had dissipated.

As for his purported involvement in a past life, I turned to my trusty companion Google to verify if there was a significant battle in France circa 1652. My research confirmed the existence of a Fronde Battle, also known as the Battle of Faubourg St Antoine, which took place during the reign of Louis XIV. Could Matt have potentially taken part in that historic event? Or was it a mere coincidence? I cannot say for certain, but what I know is that he had never set foot in France!

Following Matt's initial adventures in the realm of hypnosis, his eagerness to explore further possibilities only intensified.

Fueled by curiosity, he sought to uncover the depths of what hypnosis could achieve. We scheduled another session for two weeks later, and when the appointed time arrived, I guided Matt into a deep state of hypnosis. This time, he quickly reached a state of profound relaxation, requiring minimal time to prepare for the session ahead.

In this session, we decided to bypass the exploration of past lives and instead focused on other intriguing aspects. I invited Matt to choose any topic to discuss as he sat on the couch in a trance state, and after a long pause, he began sharing his thoughts.

> For a singularity, creating artificial intelligence, non-biological intelligence, and the whole point of biological life being just simply to create synthetic life. If all life in the universe is synthetic and biological life disappears, or at least doesn't get beyond or much beyond where we are, and then either we're trapped or killed by synthetic life, then that's why we can't see anything in the universe life-wise.

For Star Trek fans, this might evoke thoughts of the Borg. Later, I asked Matt about his recollection of the statement. He confessed to not remembering making it. At the time, ChatGPT wasn't on my radar, and "Artificial Intelligence" (AI) wasn't as much of a buzzword as it is today. ChatGPT is like a super-smart computer program developed by OpenAI, capable of conversing and writing just like a human being. Although more and more people are recognizing the benefits of using AI, concerns about its rapid advancement and its potential dangers to humanity are widespread. Could Matt's statement while under hypnosis be referring to this same concern, or was it just his imagination?

During our session, I recalled a hypnosis technique I had learned during my training, one that involved bringing one's future self into the present as a mentor. This method allows individuals to tap into their future wisdom and guidance by imagining themselves as a more knowledgeable and accomplished version of who they are today. It's like seeking counsel from your future self, who can offer insights and solutions based on their experiences and growth, providing valuable guidance for the present moment. It is having that mentor present inside of you, and you can ask for its guidance when needed.

Though I had experimented with this technique personally, I occasionally found myself frustrated by the absence of immediate answers to my questions. I thought about how convenient it would be to receive direct answers from that internal mentor, rather than waiting for solutions to emerge—a process that could take hours, days, or sometimes never happen at all!

Stage hypnotists have long used hypnosis as a source of entertainment. However, every show they present serves as a testament to the extraordinary power of the human mind and its undeniable influence on the body. Clinical hypnotists acknowledge this inherent potential and use it to assist their clients.

Countless testimonies have recounted experiences of individuals entering a hypnotic trance, followed by seemingly miraculous events. Individuals allergic to anesthetics undergoing major tooth extractions without feeling pain, patients enduring surgery while fully awake yet devoid of discomfort, individuals transforming their perspectives to ease trauma, overcome fears, and conquer phobias, athletes enhancing their performance, and individuals resolving physical conditions—the possibilities are endless!

Despite being uncertain of my next course of action, I found myself speaking calmly, almost as if on autopilot, giving him instructions before bringing him out of hypnosis. When Matt opened his eyes, they fixate on something seemingly right in front of him.

> **Matt:** It's like a floating diamond. It's like two pyramids stuck together. Four-sided pyramids. And it's slowly rotating right.
> **PM:** Where is it now?
> **Matt:** It's right there (pointing a short distance right in front of him). When I'm talking, it's like going (doing hand flashing gestures), "Bloop-boo-boo-boop!"
> **PM:** Pulsating?
> **Matt:** Yeah!
> **PM:** Ask it a question!
> **Matt:** (after a long pause) Hello?

I expected a more thought-provoking question from Matt after that prolonged pause, but anything to start an interaction at this point is welcome!

> **PM:** And... you can tell me his response.
> **Matt:** It said, "Hello."
> **PM:** Ask it another question.
> **Matt:** Um...
> **PM:** Maybe you were thinking about a decision that you're unsure about. You can ask it, it's fine. It's your mentor, it's your subconscious mind.
> **Matt:** Should I apply for jobs now, or should I apply after I come back in October?
> ... yeah, October, that makes more sense as well.
> **PM:** What did it say?
> **Matt:** It said that it thinks I should wait until I come

back from my trip, so I'm not changing the days of my trip.

PM: Okay, do you have questions you want to ask it?

Matt: Uh… should I keep wearing masks as much as possible when going outside to try to stay safe from catching Delta?

… it says, "Yes, that's the really smart thing to do."

PM: Your mentor's pretty smart!

Matt: That's what I was thinking earlier.

PM: Do you think having this mentor would be helpful to you? For when you need to ask something, you have somebody to ask?

Matt: I think so. I kind of already could do that—talk to myself—in the third person inside. I do kind of feel like I respond to myself—I think that's maybe what this is doing.

PM: Do you want me to strip it away? Or do you want to keep it? Give it a name. Do you want to give it a name, so that whenever you say that name, you will see it and it might answer you back?

Matt: (still looking at the invisible thing in front of him, before suddenly smiling) It says its name is Bosco.

PM: Nice! Do you want to keep Bosco?

Matt: Yeah, but Bosco can go away until I need him.

PM: Sure!

Matt: He says, "That's great!"

PM: Do you want Bosco to appear if you say "Bosco" if you need it?

Matt: Yeah!

Once again, I placed Matt into a hypnotic state and introduced the idea that Bosco would appear when needed and could be summoned by name. I clarified that when Bosco appeared, Matt could pose questions and possibly gain guidance or insights. Furthermore, I explained that when Bosco's presence was no longer required, he would gracefully retreat or vanish from sight. Bosco would serve as his interactive mentor, offering real-time answers and guidance in his everyday life, outside of the hypnotic state.

After the session, I inquired if Matt had any prior knowledge or familiarity with the name Bosco, to which he answered no. Matt drew a parallel between Bosco and Clippy, the Microsoft Office Assistant popular in the late '90s and early 2000s. It's an animated googly-eyed paperclip that pops up as you use the Microsoft Office program. Matt humorously pointed out that the only noticeable difference between Clippy and Bosco was that Bosco didn't constantly pester him to create a resume every time it made an appearance.

Final Thoughts and Conclusion

In this chapter, we embarked on a captivating exploration of hypnosis through Matt's real-life experiences. We explored the realms of past lives, future possibilities, and intriguing interactions with his subconscious mind. Along the way, we witnessed a remarkable phenomenon—the emergence of a floating diamond-shaped entity named Bosco, a visible representation of Matt's subconscious.

Key Insights

- Hypnosis serves as a potent tool for unlocking hidden aspects of the mind, enabling individuals to receive guidance from their subconscious.
- Matt's experiences in hypnosis showcased the vivid and realistic nature of the subconscious, where he

encountered past lives and even developed a unique mentor in Bosco.

• The subconscious mind holds invaluable insights and solutions, accessible through practice and exploration.

• Matt's encounters with his visible subconscious, represented by the floating diamond shape Bosco, revealed that the subconscious can take on distinct forms, communicate, and provide guidance in real-time, even with eyes open.

And so, a fascinating journey begins! Who could have anticipated that one's subconscious could possess a name, let alone a distinct form? Today, I witnessed the birth of an individual's visible subconscious, or as I've come to call it, a "visub." Today, I embarked on a journey into the profound recesses of someone's subconscious mind, where I encountered a presence with its very own name: a subconscious named Bosco!

2

PEELING THE VISIBLE SUBCONSCIOUS ONION

 "Imagination belongs to hope. It's the creative dance of possibility."

— *SHARON WEIL*

Matt had acquired an extraordinary ability: the power to summon Bosco into view with just a call of its name and, just as effortlessly, make it vanish. However, this left us pondering the true scope of this mysterious entity's capabilities. In the following weeks, both Matt and I persistently probed this visible subconscious, eagerly anticipating further revelations regarding its distinctive traits and potential as we continued to explore its depths.

As time passed, Bosco began revealing intriguing responses to Matt's inquiries, unveiling further facets of its nature. Meanwhile, Matt and I collaborated to decipher the factors affecting Bosco's visibility and behavior.

Our communication progressed using a widely used phone chat program over the ensuing weeks and months, serving as the medium for our informal exchanges. Below are excerpts from these dialogues, documenting our continued exploration of Matt's visible subconscious.

August 17, 2021

PM

How's Bosco?

MATT

I haven't thought about him much lately. He seems faded, less real.

PM

More faded than usual?

MATT

Yeah, or somehow muted.

PM

How's his voice? Does he still respond?

MATT

His voice is the same, still answers.

PM

Ask him why he's fading.

MATT

He says he's tired. Maybe I need more sleep (sent a virtual sticker saying, "I need answers!").

PM

Ha ha! Perfect Bitmoji! Lol. Ask him what he means.

MATT

He says my imagination is tired 😵. What does that mean?

PM

Very interesting!

MATT

I asked him again, he said we need more sleep. "I am really tired right now."

PM

Perhaps lack of sleep affects the way your mind works. Get more sleep and see if it changes.

MATT

I've noticed when Bosco is out, my brain feels active, like solving hard logic puzzles or focusing on work.

PM

Yes, makes sense. Both hemispheres of your brain are probably working when Bosco is there. You're using more of your processor, and he's like an app. If he fades, let's see if his voice remains and if your brain still feels engaged.

As I contemplated the brief duration of the previous tapping suggestion, a hint of concern began to surface. Would the visibility of the subconscious turn out to be a fleeting phenomenon? Well, we'll just have to wait and see. Hopefully, as we continue our exploration, we'll uncover more about it along the way.

August 18, 2021

PM

How was your day today?

MATT

It was cool and fun. Bosco says hi!

PM

He did? Aw... what a surprise! 🙂 Hi Bosco! How's he today? What does he look like?

MATT

Yeah, he looks more solid today.

PM

Cool! I guess when your subconscious is tired, it affects him. How about in Virtual Reality (VR)?

MATT

Same, like a semi-transparent overlay.

PM

Does he appear like a character there? I want my own Bosco! Lol.

MATT

No, just like usual, not CGI.

PM

Can you draw me a rough sketch of him sometime?

MATT

Sure!

After a few minutes, Matt sent me a picture of his sketch to my phone.

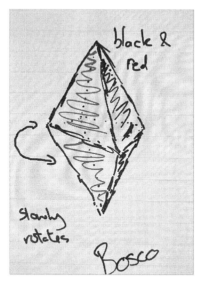

Drawing of Bosco, floating in the air and slowly rotating

MATT

He says hi again. Yeah, he lights up! I asked him if he could light up, and he did. The red panes light up!

PM

Really? That's so awesome!!! Is it a steady light? You're probably the only one (or a few) on earth who has that.

MATT

It's a steady glowing light. He can flash it, too!

August 24, 2021

PM

I'm supposed to go with a group to see the Mariners game for the first time, but I can't make it because I don't feel well. 😔 Is there anything else new with Bosco?

MATT

Oh nice! I've been to three or four Mariners games. It's always a blast! No more new Bosco stuff. Oh, I saw a ghost the other day.

PM

At least no new discoveries yet. Really? How?

MATT

I was driving by the hospital late, and out of the corner of my eye, I saw a woman in a white gown walking to the crossing. I turned my head to look at her properly and started braking, but she wasn't there in my center vision. The whole thing probably lasted a second. Was weird!

PM

Oh, gee whiz! You saw the white lady!!! It's a pretty popular sighting. Was it the first time you encountered a ghost?

MATT

I've felt presences before. First time seeing something.

PM

Did you ask Bosco what it was?

MATT

He thinks it was a ghost, too.

PM

Creepy! Hey, ask Bosco to sing you a song if he can do that.

MATT

... Bosco sang, "Daisy Daisy" the way HAL sang it in 2001!

PM

Really? That's sooo cool! Was it in your voice? LOL.

MATT

No, HAL's voice.

PM

He could do that? Nice! Did he choose the song? What did you say to him?

MATT

He did. All I said was, "Can you sing a song?" And he sang that. And it got all slow, like with HAL, like he was being deactivated.

PM

Nice! Now, there's something new that he can do—sing a song in that song's voice!

August 28, 2021

Matt and I shared a ride to the bowling alley. As we halted at a red traffic light, my curiosity sparked. I couldn't resist asking about Bosco's presence. With confidence, Matt exclaimed, "Bosco!" His gaze locked on to the center of the dashboard, pointing towards it. In that moment, Bosco materialized, hovering mid-air, slowly pirouetting. Matt remarked, "He's right there, floating and spinning." I couldn't help but wish I could witness this spectacle too.

Upon arriving at the bowling center, we noticed that many in the crowd, including ourselves, had chosen not to wear masks. Although mask mandates were lifted, COVID-19 cases were still widespread. We played two games and then left.

After a few days, Matt informed me that he was feeling unwell.

September 4, 2021

PM

How are you feeling today? Better?

MATT

No, still feeling bad. How was the movie?

PM

Aw... sorry to hear. The movie was awesomeness! And the cinema was full!!!

Ask Bosco to do a full diagnosis of your body, tell you what organs are affected, what's happening, and what you should do or take to make it better.

MATT

I'm lying in bed, catching up on Rick and Morty. Ah, cool.

PM

Ha ha! Nice! Hey, sorry to bother you, but what did Bosco say about my questions earlier? I'm curious because I don't have my own.

MATT

He said tonsils, lungs, head. He says it's viral tonsillitis. I took a COVID test, so we'll see what it says.

PM

Did he say anything about what you need to take or do to make it better?

MATT

He says sleep and flu meds are best.

PM

Ah.

MATT

He also said, "Get a COVID test."

PM

When will you get the test result?

MATT

I'm not sure; it was a 24- or 48-hour lab, so maybe tomorrow, but given it was the end of the day on a Saturday, and Monday is a holiday, I suspect Tuesday.

PM

I hope it's not COVID. I hope I don't get sick, too, if it's COVID. Good thing we already had the shot, so it won't hit that hard.

MATT

Yeah, I wasn't sick until Thursday, so hopefully you're okay. You would feel ill by now, probably.

PM

It usually takes one to two weeks before someone feels it, doesn't it? I hope I'll be fine. Need to be in San Francisco this Thursday.

If ever I get sick, I won't blame you 😊. Just treat me to a movie, and I'm good! Ha ha! (jokingly)

MATT

I'm pretty sure it's just what my kids had, but I will let you know as soon as I hear back.

Done!

PM

Cool, cool!

I'm intrigued by Bosco's response to Matt's inquiry about which part of his body was affected and what might be happening, as well as the suggested remedies. Could Bosco have been already familiar with those symptoms and conditions, or was its response influenced by the way the question was phrased?

In the spring of 2022, I stumbled upon the book *There is a River,* which narrates the life of Edgar Cayce. In the book, Sugrue (1997) recounts how Edgar experienced aphonia, a condition marked by the loss of voice often linked to vocal cord paralysis. Despite multiple doctors' efforts, none could remedy his condition until someone posed the right questions and offered suitable suggestions to Edgar while he was in a trance state.

Remarkably, physical evidence soon followed, as the color of Edgar's throat transitioned from pink to deep rose to a vivid red, before returning to its normal state. Upon awakening, Edgar found himself miraculously cured.[1] This example vividly illustrates the astonishing influence of the subconscious mind on the body.

September 6, 2021

MATT
Hey, it's not COVID!!! (test results)

PM
Nice!

October 17, 2021

PM
Goooood morning!!!!! How's it going? Excited?

MATT
Morning! I'm good, excited for sure. There are 34 hours left before I leave. Got to get packed, do laundry, etc.

PM

Woo-hoo! Excited for you! Oh, I have a tiny question.

MATT

Sure.

PM

Uh—is Bosco still alive?

MATT

Yup. He just appeared. He says hi!

PM

Oh, cool! When was the last time he appeared before today?

MATT

Um... a few days ago, I think.

PM

Ah, sweet! Hi Bosco! Did he pop up at random?

MATT

Yeah, I was stressed and thinking through things, and he showed up.

PM

Did you ask him questions about some things you were thinking through?

MATT

A little. He gave me some general advice and said what I was doing was right.

PM

Did that help in any way? How did the coding test go, by the way?

MATT

It was kind of helpful. He reminded me of a few things I'd forgotten about. I postponed it until after my trip.

PM

That's nice. I'm glad he's helpful.

MATT

😃 Thank you for giving him to me.

PM

You're welcome!

December 23, 2021

PM: Did you have a chance to consult Bosco for assistance with making healthy choices?
Matt: Yeah, I did, but then I sort of brushed it off. I could have reached out to him for help, and he was willing, but I ended up thinking I wanted to do something more, so I stopped. With my parents around and it's Christmas... yeah, I was terrible!

I was bogged down by work stress and decided to take a break. But now, I'm gearing up to get back on track, right after Christmas, maybe even before New Year's. You know, the idea was to start building a habit before the New Year begins. I figured if I start now, it'll become routine by then. They say repetition breeds habit. So, I decided to gift myself a habit for Christmas. Then, come New Year's, the resolution is to commit to sticking with it. Over the next year, I'm aiming to shed 50 pounds, which averages out to about a pound a week. It sounds doable, right?

I've realized that to get back on the weight loss track, I need to make tangible changes. For instance, if I exercise daily and cut out the junk—like sugary treats—I should lose about a pound a week without having to fret over meal plans. I don't obsess over portion sizes much, but if I just focus on cutting out the sweets and staying consistent with exercise, that alone should result in steady weight loss. That's roughly a pound per week in terms of calorie counting.

Then, I'll ramp up the exercise routine gradually. Maybe start with 20-30 minutes a day, though I prefer 45 minutes. And aim for about four workouts a week, alongside ditching sweets and managing portion sizes. That's when I can expect to see a drop of two, maybe even three pounds per week, depending on how disciplined I am.

I've fallen off the wagon before, but when I've committed, I've seen results. Once, I lost 10 pounds! But then life got in the way—I came back from vacation, work piled up, my parents visited, and it all went out the window. Now, I'm determined to pick up where I left off.

PM: Sounds like a good plan. Which aspect did you ask Bosco to assist you with?

Matt: I sought help in curbing my cravings for sweets because it's my Achilles' heel. I decided to rid my house of sugary temptations entirely. Sometimes, I rely on this thing called Huel—a nutritionally balanced meal replacement. It's convenient and takes the hassle out of meal prep. You just mix it with hot water, and voila! It's portion-controlled, so it helps with calorie management.

The plan is to have it for breakfast and lunch, then a proper dinner, and maybe some snacks. But here's the thing—I get super pumped about it initially, like, "Yes! This is it!" But after a couple of weeks, I get fatigued by it because it's having the same thing with food like that. So, I asked Bosco to keep me enthusiastic about using Huel. And it worked! I'm still excited about it. I took a break over Christmas, but my aim is to lean on Bosco to motivate me to exercise and stick with Huel. And when I asked for his help in staying excited and motivated to use Huel, I felt that surge of motivation like, "Yes! Bring on the Huel!" I felt better.

PM: How did you ask Bosco? Was there anything specific you said or how you said it?

Matt: Well, I didn't want to summon him now by saying "Hey Bosco," because then he'd pop up right away. So, I just sort of told him, you know? I said, "Hey, Bosco, help keep me motivated about using Huel so I don't get fatigued by it after a couple of weeks." And I asked him to keep me excited about it. Then he goes, "Boop-boop! Boop-boop-boop!" And that's it, all good!

PM: When did you notice the effect?

Matt: It's kind of hard to explain. It's like... right away, almost, when I went to use it again. It's like when I ask for his help with something, like eating, Huel, or whatever it may be that is "Powered by Bosco," I don't physically see Bosco, but it's almost like I can see a little... well, it might sound stupid, but you know in a video game, when you unlock a new achievement and this little badge pops up with a picture and some lines around it? It's like that, but in my mind's eye. I see this overlay, like, "This part of your life is now powered by Bosco!" So, when I'm making Huel or doing something else, it's like this badge appears, and it's like, "What you're doing now is enhanced by me, Bosco!"

PM: That's fascinating!

Matt: Yeah, so, there's no Bosco actually showing up. It's more like a little reminder. And I think maybe because I also feel this warm, fuzzy feeling, like, "Oh, nice," along with that visual cue going "ping!" And then it's like, "Yes!!!" It feels good!

PM: It's like being in a real-life video game powered by Bosco!

Matt: Exactly!

Matt's deep immersion in the world of video console games and virtual reality is evident. He's well-versed in the intricacies of gaming, where badges are coveted rewards for conquering challenges and mastering levels. These virtual accolades play a crucial role in motivating players, serving as tangible symbols of achievement and providing a sense of validation for their efforts. They're like virtual pats on the back for their accomplishments.

What's truly intriguing is how Matt's subconscious mind incorporates these gaming elements. For Matt, these badges aren't just symbols; they're powerful motivators. Leveraging his familiarity with gaming symbols, they serve as visual cues within his mind, driving him toward his goals and maintaining his motivation at optimal levels. It's a fascinating fusion of gaming culture and psychological reinforcement, demonstrating the profound influence of virtual experiences on real-life behaviors.

PM: Does he still communicate with you using your voice?

Matt: No, not anymore. It's more like... you know, it's similar to having a conversation with yourself in your mind. I'm not sure if it's the same for everyone, but when I talk to myself internally, I hear my own voice responding.

So, when I ask Bosco to assist with something, there's an acknowledgment. The sounds he makes are more like beeps or subtle cues, just to acknowledge the request. He doesn't articulate as much as before; he simply acknowledges that he's received the message, I suppose.

PM: So, it's more on visual and auditory cues for yes-no responses. However, does he still offer answers when presented with more complex questions?

Matt: It seems like I receive the answer directly into my mind, expressed in my own voice.

When it's a simple "yes," he just goes, "Boop!" for a quick acknowledgment. If it's a bit more complex, he inserts the thought into my mind, and I realize, "Oh, yeah, okay."

PM: So, during your interactions with him, his response is either a beep or the answer popping into your head, indicating his reply.

Matt: Exactly.

PM: Cool! That's quite interesting!

Intriguingly, Matt's relationship with Bosco has undergone a captivating evolution, transitioning from verbal dialogue to a more nuanced exchange of thoughts and visual cues. This transformation highlights the adaptability of the subconscious, showcasing its capacity to embrace diverse modes of communication, thereby fostering a deeper bond between Matt and Bosco.

As our exploration progressed, it became increasingly apparent that Bosco was more than just a figment of Matt's imagination; it represented a gateway to unexplored realms of consciousness. Through Bosco, Matt gleaned profound insights into his own psyche, unraveling latent potentials and confronting internal conflicts directly.

Despite the uniqueness of Matt's experiences, some might question the authenticity of his accounts concerning Bosco, especially considering he was the sole observer of its presence.

Doubts may arise, suggesting he could have been fabricating or simply going along with it. While I cannot personally vouch for witnessing Bosco, I firmly believe in the genuineness of Matt's experiences. As a hypnotist, I can affirm that the probability of Matt perceiving something is notably high. Transient suggestions of hallucinations rarely persist, yet Matt has been interacting with Bosco for over three months, underscoring the profound impact of the subconscious on an individual's perception of reality.

In his renowned book, *The Power of Your Subconscious Mind*, Murphy (1997) asserted that the remarkable secret held by great individuals throughout history resided in their capacity to tap into and release the potential of their subconscious. Importantly, Murphy emphasized that anyone could attain this accomplishment.[2]

Now, after roughly a quarter of a century, we've reached a milestone: the revelation of the visible subconscious—a revolutionary tool comparable to a master key, unlocking the limitless potential harbored within the recesses of the subconscious mind!

Final Thoughts and Conclusion

Peeling back the layers of the visible subconscious revealed a tapestry of complexities, intertwining imagination with reality and unveiling the enigmatic depths of human consciousness. Our journey with Bosco served as a testament to the untapped reservoirs of creativity and insight that lie dormant within each of us, waiting to be awakened.

In this chapter, we went deeper into the intriguing phenomenon of the visible subconscious, personified by Bosco. Matt's extraordinary ability to summon and interact with Bosco continued to evolve, shedding light on the unique traits and potential of this enigmatic entity. The exchanges between Matt and Bosco unveiled several fascinating aspects of its nature, including its responsiveness to inquiries and its ability to provide guidance and motivation.

Key Characteristics of the Visible Subconscious

- **Summoning and Disappearance:** Matt could summon Bosco with a simple call of its name and make it vanish just as easily, highlighting the entity's transient nature.
- **Influence of Sleep:** The visibility and clarity of Bosco appeared to be influenced by Matt's sleep patterns, suggesting a connection between mental energy and its manifestation.
- **Conscious Interaction:** Bosco displayed signs of consciousness by responding to questions, offering advice, and even singing.
- **Motivation and Support:** Matt harnessed Bosco's influence to motivate himself, particularly in making healthy choices and forming habits. The entity acted as a source of encouragement and motivation, enhancing his commitment to certain goals.
- **Visual and Auditory Indicators:** When Matt calls on Bosco to appear and asks questions, Bosco's responses varied, from simple beeps as acknowledgments to thoughts appearing in Matt's head for longer answers. It communicated in a way that aligned with the nature of the query.

Reflecting on our journey, I couldn't help but marvel at the profound implications of this discovery. What began as a simple experiment has blossomed into a profound exploration of the limitless capabilities of the human mind.

But can others undergo experiences similar to Matt's encounters? What additional capabilities does a visible subconscious possess? In what alternative forms can it manifest? The upcoming chapter may provide additional insights into these questions.

3

WHEN WHAT APPEARS, DISAPPEARS

 "The biggest risk is not taking any risk... in a world that's changing really quickly, the only strategy that is guaranteed to fail is not taking risks."

— *MARK ZUCKERBERG*

Can you recall a specific instance when you stubbed your toe, pricked your finger, or accidentally bumped into something, and all you desired was for that throbbing or lingering pain to cease? Wouldn't it be convenient if you could simply activate your visible subconscious and request a reduction in pain?

The subconscious mind holds the potential to influence various physiological functions, including heart rate, breathing, immune responses, and even pain perception. This chapter explores the potential of programming the subconscious mind to regulate pain intensity for individuals with a visible subconscious. It introduces an alternative manifestation of a visub and reveals a case where it abruptly ceases to exist.

One such case involves Liam, a health industry professional in his late twenties who leads an active lifestyle. Achieving a deep state of relaxation proved challenging for Liam during the session. If a mind racing at 150 miles per hour violates the speed limit, I would have given him a speeding ticket on the spot!

However, with each subsequent attempt, Liam grew increasingly relaxed and went deeper into the state of hypnosis. On the third try, he reached a profound level of relaxation and responded positively to the suggestibility test.

I proposed that upon reaching the count of three, he would open his eyes and observe my hand emitting light, and as I moved my hand, he would perceive changing colors. When Liam opened his eyes, he immediately fixed his gaze on my right hand, which was open-palmed and raised in front of him. He followed its movement intently. When asked what he was witnessing, he responded, "light." He was ready for the next phase.

Under hypnosis, I provided Liam the instructions on how to materialize his visible subconscious. This time, I chose a slightly different set of words and approach compared to what I used to summon Bosco, aiming to test its effectiveness. Below is the transcript of the hypnosis session:

> **PM:** Please describe what you see.
> **Liam:** It's a shade of grayish-white, lacking texture, with intricate lines and circles resembling a cloud.
> **PM:** Ask for its name, Liam.
> **Liam:** What's your name?
> ... it's saying it doesn't have a name.
> **PM:** It doesn't have a name? Let's give it one.
> **Liam:** Richard.

PM: Where do you sense Richard's presence? Approximately how far away is he from you?

Liam: He's probably... it, I guess... around that chair.

PM: Approximately how far?

Liam: Around 3 and a half feet.

PM: That's good. Now, ask Richard if he is your subconscious mind.

Liam: Richard, are you my subconscious mind? ... he says yes.

PM: What does Richard's voice sound like to you?

Liam: Very deep.

PM: Can you compare it to anything?

Liam: Deeper than mine.

PM: Does it resemble your voice, only deeper?

Liam: Echoey, kind of.

PM: Let's see what Richard can do. Ask what he's capable of, but use your mind only.

Liam: What can you do, Richard? ... he says he controls or is part of my thinking, even if I'm not the one thinking it. That's all he said.

PM: Now, in your mind, ask, "Can you sing a song?"

Liam: He says yes.

PM: Ask Richard to sing something... what did he sing? What sort of music?

Liam: I don't know the song's name, but it's alternative rock. I know I've heard it before.

PM: Okay. Can you tell me next time when you remember?

Liam: Yes.

PM: And when Richard sang that song, did he sound like the original singer, or did it come out in his voice?

Liam: It was his voice.

PM: Alright. Was his rendition any good?

Liam: (chuckling) I was going to say original! Now, he looks faded.

PM: How faded would you say he is at the moment?

Liam: About 50%, if we're talking in percentages.

PM: Hmmm... interesting. Ask Richard why he's fading.

Liam: Richard, why are you fading?

... I'm not getting an answer.

PM: Hmmm... okay, let's modify that.

I guided Liam back into a hypnotic state to see if we can make Richard more solid. While in this state, I also introduced the idea of pain management to his subconscious. However, I intentionally refrained from suggesting the complete elimination of pain, ensuring that Liam's body remains attuned to potential harm through pain sensation.

Following Liam's return from the trance state, our conversation continued.

PM: Can you see Richard?

Liam: Yes.

PM: Is he more solid than before?

Liam: Definitely.

PM: Would it be alright for me to pinch you?

Liam: Yes, that's fine.

PM: (pinching Liam's right leg) Do you feel any pain?

Liam: Yes, I do.

PM: Ask Richard to reduce the pain by half.

Liam: Richard, can you reduce the pain by half?

PM: And... do you feel it reduced to half?

Liam: Yes.

PM: Alright, now I'm going to pinch your other leg, and this time, it'll be firmer. (pinching Liam's left leg firmly) Do you feel pain?

Liam: Uh-huh. Yes.

PM: Ask Richard to reduce it to 1.

Liam: Richard, reduce it to 1... he says, "Okay."

PM: What's happening with the pain in your leg now?

Liam: It's probably around 1.

PM: Around 1. That's excellent!

This demonstration highlights how the visible subconscious, represented by Richard, can effectively reduce minor pain when directed to do so. According to a meta-analysis cited in a National Library of Medicine article (Thompson, T. et al., 2019), which analyzed 85 controlled trials involving 3,632 participants, hypnosis has shown significant effectiveness in reducing pain across all measures. The study found that the effectiveness of hypnosis is influenced by hypnotic suggestibility and direct analgesic suggestion, with high and medium suggestible individuals experiencing clinically meaningful reductions in pain (42% and 29% respectively). These findings suggest that hypnosis, particularly when combined with direct suggestion, offers effective pain relief and may serve as a safe alternative to pharmaceutical interventions. [1]

Before concluding the day's session, I instructed Liam to continue interacting with Richard beyond that day.

PM: Let Richard know he's free to leave.

Liam: Richard, you're free to go.

PM: Did he disappear?

Liam: Yes, he vanished.

PM: Call him back again.

Liam: Richard, come back!

PM: Can you see him now?

Liam: Yes, he's back.

PM: Alright, that's good! Now you have a friend! 😊

Afterward, when I asked Liam to draw what Richard looked like, he attempted to depict him based on our session. He sketched what he described as resembling a cloud, with clusters of clouds on its sides and additional cloud formations surrounding it. Liam noted that the edges were smooth.

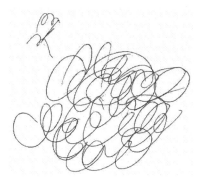

Drawing of Richard, made of clumps of clouds

A WEEK LATER, IT WAS TIME TO FOLLOW UP WITH LIAM regarding the status of his visible subconscious. As our discussion progressed, I inquired about his experience with Richard. Liam's response weighed heavily in the room, as he informed me that Richard had not returned since that day, leaving a void like that of a newfound friend suddenly vanishing. I assured Liam that together, we would explore the possibility of re-establishing his visible subconscious.

Similar to our previous sessions, Liam's analytical mind raced ahead, prompting me to metaphorically issue another speeding ticket. While Liam was in a hypnotic state, I employed a simple, yet telling test, that I call the lucidity test. This involved suggesting the presence of an insect, animal, or object in front of Liam while he remained under hypnosis. His ability to visualize it as if they were physically present would indicate a level of trance state ideal for accessing the visible subconscious. Liam struggled to clearly visualize the butterfly I suggested, yet he described the hummingbird with vivid detail, describing its black and green hues, its appearance, and its position. However, when I suggested the same visualization with his eyes open, he couldn't perceive anything.

In our previous session, Liam had discerned cloud-like shapes within his visible subconscious. Despite their lack of clarity, he could interact with the image to some extent, prompting me to contemplate the underlying mechanisms at play. The gears in my head were turning. After a brief moment of reflection, I decided it was time to explore a different approach. I repeated the same words that had summoned Bosco, but this time, instead of instructing Liam to observe his subconscious with his eyes open, I encouraged him to visualize it with his eyes closed.

I gently guided Liam out of the trance state, and as he returned to awareness, the air in the room seemed charged with anticipation. Here's a glimpse into our session:

PM: How close is it to you?
Liam: Very close.
PM: Like... within a foot?
Liam: Even less.
PM: How would you describe its size?
Liam: If it were right in front of me with my eyes open, it would fill my entire visual field. So, it's like inches away from my face.
PM: I see. And what about its color?
Liam: It's very dark... but I can make out the ridges. It looks like a brain.

PM: Uh-huh.

Liam: But I can only see the front. I can't see the sides, just the front right.

PM: Okay. Let's ask it to move a little further back so you can see it entirely.

Liam: It's shifted slightly backward.

PM: Can you see the whole thing now?

Liam: I can see more of it, but it's still like the front view. The angle only allows me to see the front and the lower portion.

PM: I understand. Have you asked if it has a name?

Liam: Yes, it doesn't respond.

PM: Okay let's give it a moment... now, mentally greet it.

Liam: ...

PM: Did you get a response?

Liam: It's like it's bobbing or levitating.

PM: I see.

Taking a moment, I provided Liam with hypnotic suggestions to foster better interaction with his subconscious mind.

PM: Is it in the same position?

Liam: It's further back, and now it appears illuminated around it.

PM: Interesting. Now, try saying hello again.

Liam: ...

PM: Are you getting a response this time?

Liam: It's hard to tell. I'm not sure if I'm hearing my own thoughts. (This observation is similar to what Matt mentioned during his session.)

PM: That's fine. Let's ask if it has a name once more.

Liam: Still no response.

PM: Let's wait a few moments. (10 seconds pass) Now, ask if it's willing to converse with you.

Liam: It's moving up and down, like nodding, but it doesn't speak.
PM: Ask it if that's its way of saying yes.
Liam: It's bobbing again.

This somehow feels like encountering a new species of intelligent life and establishing a common understanding of what a "yes" or "no" signifies in its language during the initial contact!

PM: Okay. Describe what you're seeing now.
Liam: It's back to being shadowed and even closer than before.
PM: I see. Ask it a question.
Liam: I asked if it's for real. It didn't respond, just remained there.

Compared to Matt's experience, Liam's visible subconscious seems less communicative, almost shy. It doesn't readily disclose its name but communicates through gestures. I guided Liam to deepen his relaxation state before continuing our session.

Liam: It's the same as before, but slightly further back.
PM: Alright. Ask it anything.
Liam: It's just hovering there.
PM: Tell Richard it's alright to communicate.
Liam: It replied, almost in my voice, "I know, but I don't feel like it."
PM: Okay. Inquire why.
Liam: It says it doesn't need to.
PM: Understood. Now think of a question. Maybe you have a choice to make, and you're not sure which one to choose.

Liam: ... I asked something, but it said, "You already know the answer to it."

PM: May I ask what the question was?

Liam: I asked it, "Since we started doing the hypnosis, do I feel okay now?" (Before this project, I worked with Liam briefly to resolve a long-standing issue he struggled with.)

PM: And what's your take on that?

Liam: I think the answer is yes.

PM: Okay. Ask if it has a specific name.

Liam: It responded, "I am you."

PM: Does it have a distinct name?

Liam: It simply said, "You."

PM: Alright. Ask what else it can do for you.

Liam: ... no clear answer. It said, "Whatever we need to do," but it wasn't specific. And not "we" as in you and me, but "we" as in it and I.

PM: I understand. Ask if it can manage pain, perhaps reduce it when requested.

Liam: ... it's unsure.

PM: Okay. Ask it if it's willing to appear even outside hypnosis, visually accessible when called on.

Liam: It replied, "I will try."

PM: Alright.

I instructed Liam to open his eyes to check if he could see his subconscious form. Unfortunately, the visible subconscious remained resistant to revealing itself when Liam's eyes were open. This is reminiscent of Laura's similar challenge, where she could not see her visible subconscious with eyes open but could clearly see it with her eyes closed.

PM: Let's try a different approach. I want you to reach out to your higher mind or subconscious and ask how it wants to be perceived. What can you do to make it visible?

Liam: It says it prefers not to be visible.

PM: Understandable. Can you ask why it doesn't want to be visible?

Liam: It's not entirely clear, but it suggests that I can see it when my eyes are closed.

PM: Alright. Does it mean that whenever you close your eyes and call upon "Liam," you'll see it, even after our session?

Liam: It says, "Yes."

PM: Does it speak in your voice, or does it sound different?

Liam: It sounds like mine.

PM: Understood. Now, let's try something else. Ask it to make you feel warm, like you are wrapped in a nice, cozy blanket. (It's a cold December in Washington State; the room heater broke and the oil heater was taking its time to heat the entire room.)

Liam: (after a pause) I don't feel warm.

PM: What did it say when you asked?

Liam: It said, "You do feel warm." It mentioned feeling warmth in some areas but not others. For instance, my hand feels cold, but everything under my clothes feels warm.

PM: Okay. Ask it to focus on warming the colder areas of your body to make it feel comfortable.

Liam: It says it is trying to.

PM: Let me know if you notice any changes in sensation on your hands.

Liam: (after a long pause) It does feel slightly warmer, but my fingers are still cold.

PM: Let's give it a bit more time.

After waiting, I placed my palm slowly on his lower arm, and even before lightly touching it, I could feel the warmth emanating from it. That warmth was non-existent in the finger areas. When I touched his fingers, they were noticeably cold.

> **P.M.:** Perhaps it's still working on your fingers to make it warm. (giving it around 20 seconds) How do your fingers feel now?
> **Liam:** A bit warmer.
> **PM:** Good. I'll touch your fingers to check. (Touching the fingers and feeling the warmth, then touching the tips of his fingers and noticing that they still felt cold). Alright, let's give it a bit longer to work on your fingers (long pause). Can you see your visible subconscious clearly?
> **Liam:** Yes.

As the session progressed, Liam described his visible subconscious with increasing clarity and detail, remarking on its evolving appearance and behavior.

> **PM:** Can you see your visible subconscious clearly now?
> **Liam:** Yes, I can.
> **PM:** Is it distinct?
> **Liam:** Absolutely. It feels much more real than before. It's like I'm seeing it clearer now!
> **PM:** That's progress!
> **Liam:** Definitely. But it's quite strange-looking, almost ominous. It resembles a brain, but the coloring is eerie. It's as if the prefrontal cortex is staring at me without eyes. And it remains static, just there in the darkness. But I can see the gyri—where the folds of the brain are. And while we're still doing the session, I could literally say, "Okay, go further away." "Come closer." Originally,

no, it was literally just right here (placing his hand about six inches from his face to show how close it was). Then, we did something, and then it moved further out. And towards the end of the session, it was away out there (pointing to one end of the room). I could call it closer, but not close enough again until it was like (putting a hand near his face), right here.

PM: Fascinating. You were able to adjust its distance during the session.

Liam: Yes, I could command it to move closer or further away.

PM: Interesting. And when it communicates with your voice, you feel like it's you speaking to yourself?

Liam: Exactly. It's like a part of me, so there's a natural connection.

PM: That's a common experience. And your subconscious prefers not to show itself visually?

Liam: Right. It's almost like it's protecting itself, which makes sense given my tendency to keep things private. At one point, I remember you telling me to relax to get me into a deeper state, and it was in color for a bit. It was like a pink brain. I don't know if, perhaps, I like it better dark, so it switched back.

Another thing I noticed was, once I could see it, I had no other thoughts in my head! No part of my imagination was wandering on a different thing, it was stuck on that!

PM: Indeed. And it seems to identify as you, without the need for a separate name.

Liam: Exactly. It's an extension of myself, so there's no need for formalities.

PM: Understood. And your hands?

Liam: My hands were generally cold, but when you started telling me to warm it up, the sensation was weird, like it only went to the middle of my hand. My fingertips are always cold! Prior to that, my hands were freezing, but I felt a warming sensation particularly in the fingers.

PM: It seems like your subconscious is adapting to your needs.

Liam: Absolutely! It's a work in progress, but I'm impressed by its efforts!

I purposefully refrained from sharing detailed accounts of participants' experiences with each other unless they had already encountered similar situations and were actively seeking clarification or examples. This approach enabled me to identify commonalities in the participants' encounters more accurately. By allowing each individual's experience to unfold organically and without external influence, I could observe unique patterns and responses, contributing to a richer understanding of the subconscious exploration process.

Final Thoughts and Conclusion

In this chapter, we delved deeper into the enigmatic realm of the visible subconscious, unearthing intriguing insights into its nature and capabilities. As we journeyed through the experiences of Liam, a health industry professional, and his interactions with his visible subconscious, we uncovered several remarkable facets of this phenomenon.

Key Insights

- **Adaptability of the Visible Subconscious:** One key takeaway is the visible subconscious's remarkable adaptability. It can assume forms and behaviors that resonate with the individual's inner psyche. In Liam's case, it took on the appearance of a brain, reflecting his intellectual curiosity and fascination with human anatomy. After all, the subconscious has a knack for drawing upon the things that matter most to the individual it belongs to.

- **Intimate Connection:** Our exploration revealed the intimate connection between the individual and their visible subconscious. Communication often involves a voice that sounds remarkably similar to the individual's own, blurring the lines between self and subconscious. This sense of familiarity and self-resemblance adds complexity to the relationship with one's inner mind. It, however, suggests a distinction, indicating that the source of the reply emanates from their visible subconscious mind.

- **Practical Applications:** We discovered the practical applications of the visible subconscious, particularly in pain management. Through hypnotic suggestions, individuals can modulate pain intensity, offering therapeutic potential in alleviating physical discomfort. In this case, it is requesting the visible subconscious to decrease pain.

- **Can Be a Reserved Entity:** Each person is unique, and this uniqueness suggests a distinct connection between the subconscious and an individual's personality. This connection may reflect deeply private or guarded aspects of the self. In Liam's case, his visible subconscious appeared to shy away from direct communication or revealing its name.

- **Unanswered Questions:** As we conclude this chapter, numerous questions remain unanswered. The experiences of various participants, including Liam, have enriched our understanding of the visible subconscious, yet mysteries and possibilities abound.

In our journey of discovery, the visible subconscious continues to captivate our imagination and challenge our understanding of the human psyche. It serves as a reminder that the depths of our minds are vast and uncharted, harboring untold secrets and untapped potential that we are only just beginning to fathom.

As this chapter concludes, tantalizing questions about the visible subconscious linger. What further abilities might it possess? How does it adapt to the unique characteristics and life experiences of each individual? Liam's exploration has added depth to our exploration, leaving us eager to uncover more about this remarkable phenomenon. With each participant's journey, we edge closer to further unraveling the intricate connections between the mind, identity, and the visible subconscious.

In the upcoming chapter, we will continue to explore the mysteries of the visible subconscious, with Bosco taking center stage to offer fresh insights and perspectives on this captivating enigma.

4

MATT'S EXPERIENCE: HARNESSING THE HEALING POWER WITHIN

> *"Believe in the power of truth... do not allow your mind to be imprisoned by majority thinking. Remember that the limits of science are not the limits of imagination."*
>
> — DR. PATRICIA E. BATH

Hypnosis has a rich history in the medical field, with documented use dating back to both World War I and World War II. It demonstrated effectiveness in relieving pain, diminishing the requirement for anesthesia, and assisting soldiers during surgical procedures. In addition to its wartime uses, hypnosis played a vital role in treating post-traumatic stress disorder (PTSD) during World War II.

Today, hypnosis is increasingly recognized within the medical community, as practitioners seamlessly incorporate it into their practice and clinical studies broaden the scope of its applications.

Hypnosis has been applied notably in reducing hospital anxiety among children with cancer (Talebiazar et al., 2022).[1]

Additionally, hypnotherapy and targeted medical hypnosis have made their way into the realms of surgical and emergency medicine (Speigel, 2011).[2] Moreover, Bourmault and Anteby (2023) shed light on the intriguing case of French anesthesiologists successfully incorporating hypnosis as an effective alternative to general anesthesia in the operating room (OR).[3]

Three months have passed since Bosco's birth as a visible subconscious, and I must admit, I'm thoroughly impressed with how consistently visible and responsive he has been to Matt and myself.

Throughout my time working with Bosco, I haven't delved into the realm of pain management. I've pondered the notion of "programming" Bosco to handle pain, similar to what was done with Liam. However, Liam's visible subconscious also exerted its influence on other bodily functions, such as causing certain parts of his body to feel warm.

This got me wondering if Bosco could possess similar abilities. With a handful of ideas in my mind, I saw this upcoming session as the perfect opportunity to go deeper into this fascinating exploration.

Matt and I met one morning and as we entered the office, he settled on the couch, our designated space for hypnosis sessions.

Two weeks prior, Matt had confided in me about his work-related distress, which had led to symptoms resembling panic attacks for several days. Fortunately, he's now in a better state, having parted ways with that job, and was eagerly anticipating his COVID-19 booster shot later that day.

Before plunging Matt into trance, I hesitated, contemplating the possibility of conducting a pain management test with Bosco. The objective was to determine whether Bosco possessed the ability to manage pain without first inducing hypnosis in Matt.

> **PM:** Alright, before we go into the hypnosis session, I'd like to conduct a few tests with Bosco. Could you summon him, please?
>
> **Matt:** Bosco!
>
> … he's right over there (pointing to the space above the microwave oven)!
>
> **PM:** Where? Here? (Extending my right hand a few inches above the microwave oven positioned a few feet in front of Matt.)

Matt rose from his chair, his left hand outstretched, pointing toward a spot just beyond my reach as he described Bosco's appearance.

Intrigued by its size, I inquired, and Matt gestured with his hands, as if cradling a figure about a foot and a half tall. "It's about this big!" he exclaimed enthusiastically before settling back onto the couch.

> **PM:** Cool! Okay, ask Bosco if he can control or manage pain.
>
> **Matt:** (looking at the space above the microwave) Bosco, can you manage pain? … he says he can try.
>
> **PM:** Alright, I'll pinch you on your left leg and then ask Bosco to reduce the pain by half (pinching Matt's left leg firmly to ensure he feels the pain).
>
> **Matt:** Bosco, reduce the pain by half! … he says, "Okay."
>
> **PM:** Can you describe how it felt?
>
> **Matt:** Yeah! So, I felt the pinch. Then it's like it got numb, and I felt pressure, and it felt a bit warm. Eventually, the pain fell away quite fast!

PM: Okay, and when I asked you to reduce it by half?

Matt: It still felt like a pinch, but less intense.

PM: So, it felt like only half of the pain?

Matt: Yeah!

PM: That's good! Yay, we discovered something new! Now, let's explore something else. I'm considering anesthesia. Some people can't have it due to allergies, so they turn to hypnosis to numb areas like the gums, similar to anesthesia. Let's see if Bosco can do something similar. Maybe ask him to numb a part of your body, like the gums or a finger, just for testing.

Matt: How about this finger? (moving his left index finger)

PM: I don't know... let's try here (pointing to the soft area between the left index finger and thumb). I'll pinch this spot (drawing a small circle on the area with my index finger). Alright, ask Bosco to make this area numb!

Matt: Hey, Bosco, can you make this area numb? ... he says, "Okay."

PM: (pinching the area)Do you feel any pain?

Matt: A little bit.

PM: Only a bit?

Matt: Yeah, it's more like pressure and tingling.

PM: Got it (pinches the area again). Still pinching your left hand.

Matt: It's like pressure and tingle.

PM: Pressure and tingle. Okay, let's leave it for a few more seconds. I don't know how long it would take. When someone injects you with anesthesia, it usually takes a couple of seconds to take effect. I'm not sure if it's the same thing with this.

Matt: It felt like I really didn't notice it until you

pinched. And then, as soon as you pinched, there was a bit of pain, and it quickly went away.

PM: Got it.

Matt: So, it's like it didn't take effect until the pain was present, I guess?

PM: (pinching the area again) How about now?

Matt: There's more pain again, but not as intense.

PM: Ask Bosco to numb it, just as if you had anesthesia on it.

Matt: Hey, Bosco? Make this area numb as if I have anesthesia on it (circling the area on his left hand with his right index finger) ... he says, "Okay."

PM: Alright. And ask him if it's ready... how long does it take?

Matt: (directed at Bosco) Is it numb? ... he says, "yes."

PM: He says yes, okay (pinching the area again).

Matt: I just feel pressure.

PM: No pain?

Matt: Just pressure.

PM: I'm pinching it now here (moving to a slightly adjacent area on the skin, pinching, and moving a little further each time toward where the index finger and thumb meet). Pinching... pinching... pinching...

Matt: The pinch on this area was just pressure. The last pinch felt painful there (pointing to the spot where I pinched last, just outside the outlined area).

PM: Ah, that's because you outlined the numbed area with your finger earlier, and the last pinch was just outside of it.

Bosco effectively numbs an area on Matt's left hand upon request, allowing him to feel the pressure of my pinches without experiencing pain, until I pinched outside of that area.

As the experiment progressed, I noticed the skin on Matt's hand had turned reddish due to repeated pinching. Additionally, I observed a bulging vein, approximately a centimeter in size, which made me somewhat uneasy. I have always had an aversion to the sight of blood, but to my dismay, I realized this afternoon that I equally despise the sight of enraged, green veins!

> **PM:** Is that your vein?
> **Matt:** Yeah. Ouch!
> **PM:** I'm so sorry!
> **Matt:** (examining it closely) Yep, maybe we burst a vein (starts laughing)!

Matt's laughter fills the room, but I'm feeling a pang of guilt, thinking I should have used a wooden clothespin or pinched a different area on his arm.

> **Matt:** It's okay, it will go away. (winces as he touches the vein) Ouch! It's only painful if I touch it.
> **PM:** How about asking Bosco to reduce the pain to one and try touching it again?
> **Matt:** Hey, Bosco? Reduce the pain in my hand to one. (pauses, then cautiously touches the vein) Yeah, okay, it's gone away!
> **PM:** So, when you touch it, you feel nothing?
> **Matt:** (touches the vein again) Nope.
> **PM:** Sorry. (I feel a bit relieved when he feels no pain.)
> **Matt:** It's okay. Yeah, hopefully, it will just go away.
> **PM:** What if you ask Bosco to heal it (I suggest this because, yes, I still feel guilty!)?
> **Matt:** Hey Bosco, can you heal my hand? ... he says he'll try.

After about three minutes, I notice that the swelling significantly subsided, and the area where the pregnant vein was now appears almost flat. My eyes widen!

PM: Hey, look at it!

Matt: The swelling's gone down a bit.

PM: Yeah... that was quick!

Matt: Maybe it's like a hematoma? It bursts, stretches, inflates a bit, then reabsorbs in a couple of days...

PM: But it went down fast! Earlier, there was a green bump where the vein was.

Matt: Yeah.

PM: Bosco's doing a great job! It's hardly noticeable now!

Matt: I think it's still there, hiding behind the red area, like blood.

PM: Hmmm.

Matt: Yeah... it's alright. I wonder how long they stay hidden. They're red now but might turn black or something.

PM: (takes a picture of the hand) Okay, I'll take another picture later. Just keep an eye on it because Bosco said he'll try to heal your hand (I realize I should have taken a pic of the hand with the inflamed vein for comparison). I remember you mentioned the incident you had at work on a Friday. Did it affect you for a couple of days?

Matt: Yeah, I felt terrible from Friday until Sunday. I just felt emotionally numb, like I was in shock. On Sunday, I got emotional and cried, which helped release all that pent-up emotion. Then, during work, I'd get moments of panic because of the stress! I don't usually have panic attacks; it's more like my anxiety spikes. But as soon as I remembered, "Oh, but it doesn't matter because I'm leaving," everything settled down.

PM: Alright, when you're experiencing something like panic attacks or anxiety, maybe you could ask Bosco to minimize or manage it. Let's see how it goes. Because the subconscious mind can have a big influence on that, too. Let me know if you're not getting the results you want, and we can attempt to program your subconscious (Bosco) with more instructions on how to manage it.

Matt: Yes, that would be interesting!

PM: So instead of going to a therapist and undergoing hypnosis, it would all go through Bosco. If you say, "Bosco, adjust the anxiety levels to..." Well, depending on the instructions I give him for managing anxiety, he'll follow them.

Matt: That would be pretty amazing! I can think of a few things, actually. Stress and anxiety are the biggest mental hurdles for me.

PM: How about asking Bosco to clear your mind of those thoughts? Experiment with that and let me know how it affects you. And if there are any habits you want to change, ask Bosco if he can help by saying something like, "Help me stop this..." or "Reduce my desire to do this..."

Matt: Yeah!!! I could have tried those a week ago when my anxiety levels were high! It would have been helpful! Wow! I haven't used Bosco much.

That's right, Matt! I gave you a Ferrari, and you've been using it to go to the supermarket! That night, I messaged Matt to check on his hand.

PM

Heya! How's your hand?

MATT

It's much better.

PM

No hematoma or marks? Any pain?

MATT

A little pain. A bruise, but it looks okay.

PM

Is it the same color/size of the bruise as earlier?

MATT

No, you can hardly see it.

PM

Nice! Glad to hear! 😄 Good job, Bosco!

After further discussion, a clearer picture emerges regarding the circumstances of Matt's work situation. It appears that his situation had significantly worsened following his vacation, prompting him to make the decision to submit his two weeks' notice.

Final Thoughts and Conclusion

In this chapter, we've scratched the surface of the visible subconscious's potential. We've seen its capability to influence our sensory perceptions and mental states. These remarkable findings raise intriguing possibilities, including speculation about the potential for expediting the healing process. This reminds me of what Dr. Dispenza (2008) said about the body being equipped with everything it needs to heal, in his book entitled *Evolve Your Brain*.[4]

As we continue our journey, we'll delve deeper into the visible subconscious' capabilities and uncover more about its unpredictable nature. Stay curious, stay open to exploration, and be prepared for further revelations in the chapters ahead.

To wrap up this chapter, let's reflect on the important points.

Key Insights

- Hypnosis has a rich history and has evolved into a valuable therapeutic tool, finding applications from pain management to anxiety reduction.
- The introduction of Bosco, a visible subconscious, added an extra dimension to the exploration of hypnosis and its capabilities.
- Through experiments with Bosco, we were able to replicate Liam's visible subconscious' ability to alter the perception of pain upon request, such as decreasing pain sensation or numbing an area of the body.
- The responsiveness of the visible subconscious to suggestions, even outside of a trance state, indicates its malleability and potential for further exploration.

5

TESTING THE LIMITS: EXPLORING THE VISIBLE SUBCONSCIOUS' INFLUENCE

 "Progress is impossible without change, and those who cannot change their minds cannot change anything."

— *GEORGE BERNARD SHAW*

In my role as a hypnotherapist, I have had the privilege of supporting clients on their weight loss journeys. Many come to me with a common objective: overcoming cravings for indulgent foods, especially junk food. Weight gain often results from various factors beyond medical conditions and genetics, including poor food choices, battling cravings, ingrained beliefs, anxiety management, and the struggle to establish consistent exercise routine.

Hypnosis emerges as a powerful tool in helping clients reprogram their minds, empowering them to opt for healthier choices, conquer cravings, manage anxiety, and ultimately increase their chances of shedding weight.

One woman shared her struggle with donuts. She admitted that whenever she visited Ikea, passing by the donut store inevitably led to a purchase. Initially intending just a single bite for the taste, she found herself devouring the entire donut, even when buying various flavors, despite desiring just one bite.

We analyzed her purchasing process and the sequence from taking a bite to finishing the entire donut. It all started with the captivating aroma of the donut, metaphorically acting like a lasso, drawing her in due to her longing for its taste.

Upon the first bite, she savored the delightful combination of a soft texture and irresistible sweetness, which strongly appealed to her palate. These sensations overwhelmed her, prompting further bites and ultimately the consumption of one or more donuts, leaving her feeling disappointed in herself.

During the hypnosis session, I suggested that after taking a bite, she could fully relish the taste and texture, finding satisfaction in that single bite. Subsequent bites would lose their appeal due to diminished taste and smell. I reassured her that leaving the donut unfinished was perfectly acceptable.

Two weeks later, she returned for a follow-up session, admitting her initial skepticism about our previous meeting's effectiveness. However, she acknowledged feeling progress and expressed interest in reinforcing the suggestions made during our last session.

This example highlights how our senses influence our behaviors, moods, and decision-making, sometimes leading us astray from what is truly beneficial. By adjusting these sensory experiences, we can better align our decisions with our desired goals.

In this chapter, we'll explore whether the visible subconscious can alter sensory perceptions without the need for hypnosis as a preliminary step.

To investigate this concept, I invited Matt to my office for a brief check-in. I informed him of a quick test involving Bosco, his visible subconscious form, without disclosing specific details. Our meeting occurred three weeks after the Fourth of July in 2022. During the check-in, I retrieved a zip-lock bag from my backpack and placed it on the table. The following transcript presents our conversation:

> **Matt:** (observing the transparent bag) A knife and a lemon!
> **PM:** Yes! I want to see if Bosco can alter some of your senses, particularly taste and smell. So, I brought this fresh lemon and a knife.
> **Matt:** (eyeing the steak knife cautiously) The knife looks threatening. Well, to me, it does!

With caution, I sliced the bright yellow lemon in two, maintaining a safe distance to avoid startling Matt. As the juice trickled onto the cutting board, my mouth watered instinctively. The refreshing scent of the lemon filled the air. Setting the knife down, I extended one of the lemon halves to Matt.

> **PM:** So, first, let's tackle the smell. We'll start by experimenting with how it smells. Ask Bosco to remove the smell or make it so you won't be able to smell it. Then we'll restore it. After that, we can move on to the taste test.
> **Matt:** Just curious: you know there are pills you can take that do that, right? (Referring to the glycoprotein-binding pill. This pill makes it so that sour food, such as lemon, appears to taste sweet.)
> **PM:** Yes! My co-worker mentioned that her family tried it, and she was amazed!

Matt: I've tried that, it worked, and it blew my mind! My freaking mind! Like, "What's happening right now?!!"

PM: Exactly! So let's begin. Smell it!

Matt: (bringing the lemon close to his nose) Smells great! Like a fresh lemon!

PM: Fresh lemon! Okay, cool! Now ask Bosco to remove the smell or alter your sense so you can't smell it.

Matt: Hey Bosco? Um... try to take away the smell of the lemon so that it smells like nothing! (He brings the lemon closer to his nose, pulls it away momentarily, then smells it again.) It still has a hint of lemon scent, but not as strong as before.

PM: How much weaker is the smell now?

Matt: (squeezing the lemon slightly and smelling it again) Only slightly, actually.

PM: But earlier, it was quite potent, right?

Matt: Yes.

PM: I noticed it earlier, too, when I sliced it.

Matt: (bringing the lemon close to his nose again) Ah, I can barely detect the scent at all now.

PM: Great! Now ask Bosco to restore the lemon's original smell.

Matt: Hey, Bosco, stop masking the smell and let me smell it normally. (Sniffing the lemon) Yeah, smells like a lemon now!

PM: Is the change in smell intensity noticeable?

Matt: Yeah, I think so. It still has that lemony aroma, but it went from being very fresh to just slightly lemony.

PM: Now let's try changing it to something else. How about asking Bosco to change the smell of the lemon to the smell of... what other fruit would you like?

Matt: Orange?

PM: Orange it is! A strong orange smell! Let me know what he says.

Matt: Okay, Bosco, make this smell like an orange! A powerful orange smell! (Squeezing the lemon before taking a whiff) Smells like tangerine!

PM: Tangerine, huh? A strong tangerine smell?

Matt: (sniffing it again) Yeah, it smells like freshly peeled tangerine. (He sniffs again, looking surprised) Yeah!

PM: Okay, now ask him to change it back to the lemon smell.

Matt: Right. Um, Bosco, make this smell like a lemon again. (Taking another whiff of the lemon) Yeah, it's lemony.

PM: Okay, back to the lemon smell.

Matt: (Nods)

PM: Excellent! So now you know he can alter the sense of smell! This applies to food too, because some people get addicted to specific foods due to their smell, influencing their taste. You can ask Bosco to change whatever you really like about something to help curb cravings.

Matt: Yeah.

PM: Or maybe enhance the taste or the smell or color of the vegetables and all that good (healthy) food, so you can eat more if you know what I mean.

Matt: Uh-huh.

PM: Cool! Now onto the next experiment—the taste change test! (Taking Matt's piece of lemon and handing him the other half). There it is! Just taste a little. A small bite of that freshly sliced lemon!

Matt: (takes a bite of the lemon) That's a sour lemon!

PM: Now, ask Bosco to change that lemon taste to... maybe a very sweet orange!

Matt: Bosco, try to change this to taste like a sweet orange, so it's not as sour (glancing at the fruit)!

PM: Did he say okay?

Matt: Yeah, he does this acknowledging-kind-of-like, "Boop, boop!" (bites on the lemon and stops) Hmmm...

PM: Still lemon?

Matt: It kind of tastes like... a bad orange! (laughs) Still kind of sour.

PM: Or... do you think it also takes time? Just like the smell test earlier, where it took a few seconds before it took effect?

Matt: (takes another bite of the lemon and looks at it) Yeah, it tastes like really strong orange juice. Really strong orange juice!

PM: A really strong orange juice—but is it sweet?

Matt: (takes another bite of the lemon) Um...

PM: Or... ask him to make it taste like sugar.

Matt: Bosco, make this taste as sweet as you can, like sugar... okay. (takes another bite out of the lemon) It's like it tastes... (seemingly unsure, takes another quick bite) so overpowering! It tastes sweet and then immediately very bitter.

PM: Oh, so the sweetness doesn't last.

Matt: No, it's like the sweet part of my tongue is going off, and it's tasting sweet. But the sour on the side is also going off, and it thinks sour. It's weird, kind of...

PM: Okay, how about asking Bosco to let all parts of your tongue taste it like it's sweet?

Matt: Hey, Bosco. Make all of my tongue think that this is something that's sweet and not a lemon. (brief pause before biting on the lemon) Um... (takes another bite. Now I could see the typical lemon-wincing face in him) That is a really strange sensation. It's like it's trying.

PM: Uh-huh.

Matt: It's like my tongue is going in waves. It's like, (starts lifting each hand up and down) "Sweet! Sour!

Sweet! Sour! Sweet! Sour!" That's weird! (has another taste)

PM: Oh, and one last thing. Could you ask Bosco if he can make it taste sweet, just like the time when you had the pill?

Matt: Bosco, can you make it seem like I had that protein-binding pill in my tongue, where my senses only detect the sweetness and not the sour? (Pausing briefly, and after seemingly getting a response, bites on the lemon. His face quickly turns very sour) That made it very sour! Oh, my gosh! That's overpowering! (pausing for a few seconds while trying to make out what it is) Ack!!! (shaking his head, his face exhibiting after-shocks of extreme sourness) That made it worse! I don't know!

As I observed Matt's facial expressions, I couldn't help but notice my own face involuntarily wincing. I then instructed him to place the lemon inside the zip-lock bag and seal it, thus concluding the Bosco lemon test.

In a Stanford Medicine article titled *Study Identifies Brain Areas Altered During Hypnotic Trances*, Williams (2016) emphasizes how altered states of consciousness enhance the brain's control over bodily functions.[1] In hypnosis, direct suggestions aimed at altering bodily functions have a significant impact. One common example is the suggestion of increased tolerance for cold and pain, demonstrated by a person submerging their hand in a bucket of iced water for several minutes, a feat they otherwise could not achieve. Another example is from a TV show where a hypnotist placed a man who wanted to test this theory into a hypnotic trance. Several of his friends watched as one of them applied a wax strip on his hairy back. When the friend suddenly pulled the strip with an audible ripping sound, his friends flinched or grimaced in discomfort at the sight, even gasping... except for the hypnotized man, lying still and quiet.

Hypnosis can influence the brain's processing of sensory information, including smell, by modulating neural pathways and perception. During a hypnotic session, a person's heightened focus and suggestibility may enable them to reinterpret or even block out certain smells. This can cause perceiving a reduced intensity of odors, altering their quality, or even changing it to a more pleasant scent. The same concept may apply to the sense of taste. This case, however, demonstrates a similar effect showing enhanced mind-body connection being carried out by the visible subconscious without putting the person in a trance state.

While outcomes can vary from person to person and the effort they put in, the results of the test closely mirror the successes I've witnessed while assisting clients in weight loss hypnosis. For some individuals, altering the intensity of taste, smell, or the texture of specific foods has proven remarkably effective in diminishing their appeal. Conversely, for others, enhancing the desirability of healthy foods becomes a viable alternative. This change often coincides with a shift in their mood or thought patterns, providing them with the means to better control their cravings. It empowers them to make conscious choices about their dietary habits.

While we might like to believe that we're always in control and that our senses can only be intentionally altered, it may surprise many to learn how our senses can be influenced without our conscious awareness. An experiment conducted at Harvard (Spence et al., 2014) revealed that the background noise on airplanes can diminish the perception of sweetness and saltiness in food. Consequently, more salt and sugar are added to airplane meals to maintain a taste experience similar to that on the ground. Strangely, the same background noise enhances the taste of umami in tomatoes, prompting an increased number of people to order Bloody Marys or tomato juice inflight—choices they wouldn't typically make.[2]

In a blog post on the National Hypnotherapy Society site (National Hypnotherapy Society, no date, as cited in *Playing with the Senses Can Change How Food Tastes*), various experiments are discussed. For instance, desserts tasted sweeter and more flavorful when served on white plates, while less junk food was consumed when presented on red plates. Additionally, playing tinkling high-pitched music enhances sweetness, while low-pitched brassy music makes bitterness more noticeable in food and drinks. Manipulating light brightness also influences food and drink choices. Similarly, red lights and sweet background music enhance the fruitiness of red wine.[3]

Final Thoughts and Conclusion

In this thought-provoking chapter, we investigated further the power of the visible subconscious and its potential to influence our sensory perceptions. Through a fascinating lemon test with Matt, we explored how Bosco, the visible subconscious, could alter the smell and taste of a lemon, showcasing the malleability of our sensory experiences. While some aspects of this control may remain enigmatic, there's no doubt about its potential in helping us make better choices in our daily lives.

Key Insights

- Hypnosis, as a therapeutic tool, can play a significant role in helping individuals overcome cravings and make healthier choices, particularly in the context of weight loss.

- Sensory experiences have a profound impact on our behaviors and decision-making processes, sometimes leading us to indulge in unhealthy habits.
- The lemon test experiment demonstrated Bosco's ability to manipulate the sense of smell, transitioning the scent from lemon to orange, and decreasing the intensity of the scent, highlighting its responsiveness to suggestions.
- While taste modification exhibited certain limitations, it offered valuable insight into the ability of the visible subconscious to influence taste perceptions, albeit with some complexity. This demonstration intentionally pushed the taste test to its limits, but the practical aspect of altering the sense of taste is more focused on enhancing or diminishing certain elements of that sense.
- Real-world applications of sensory modification in therapeutic settings such as decreasing the intensity of the food in question's perceived taste, smell, texture, or sound, have proven effective in reducing cravings and promoting healthier eating habits.

In the upcoming chapter, we'll venture further into the exploration of the visible subconscious, uncovering its elusive nature and discovering extra surprises along the way. Stay curious, stay open to possibilities, and join us in further unraveling the mysteries of the subconscious mind!

6

FINDING AN ELUSIVE SUBCONSCIOUS

 "Until the mind is open, the heart stays closed. The open mind is the key to the heart."

— *BYRON KATIE*

During a dinner meeting, Laura expressed her aspirations for a fitness routine and acknowledged the challenges it presented. In response, I shared a story about an individual who achieved unexpected help in pursuing a similar goal by engaging with their visible subconscious. Intrigued by the concept, Laura asked more questions. I proposed she volunteer to make her own subconscious mind visible and interactive. Her excitement was apparent as she eagerly agreed to take part.

Laura, a vibrant and intelligent woman in her fifties, not only prioritizes her physical fitness but also actively engages in analytical work within her profession. We planned to meet at my modest office on a laid-back Saturday afternoon.

As the day of our scheduled appointment arrived, I encountered an unexpected delay but kept Laura informed via a quick message.

> **PM:** Take your time; I'm running a few minutes late.
> **Laura:** Okay. Getting something at Starbucks. See you there.
> **PM:** Starbucks, huh? Hopefully not a coffee?
> **Laura:** Nah, just a latte.

Laura understood my intention and opted for a latte instead, avoiding coffee as initially contemplated.

As Laura settled into my office, I motioned her to take a seat, assuring her of my availability for any queries or concerns.

> **Laura:** You're not going to make me bark like a dog every time someone says bark, are you?
> **PM:** (grinning) No. Not every time.

Laura's laughter filled the room, easing any tension. After guiding Laura into relaxation using guided imagery, I posed a question, but she remained still, offering no response. Slightly raising my voice to catch her attention, I provided her with instructions for the initial test.

> **PM:** Laura. Use your excellent visualization or imagination with your eyes still closed. At the count of three, you will see a brightly colored butterfly fluttering in front of you. It will seem very real to all your senses. And you will describe it to me easily as you remain in a relaxed state. One... two... three!

Several seconds ticked by with no response. In my mind, I couldn't help but joke, "Laura, you better not have dozed off on me, or you owe me a cup of coffee!" Suddenly, her eyes started darting rapidly beneath her closed eyelids, indicating she had entered a somnambulistic state.

PM: Describe what you see.
Laura: (raising her hands as if shielding her face) It's too bright! It's too bright!

Reacting swiftly, I suggested that the brightness intensity had been lowered. I made a mental note to avoid using the combination of the words "bright" and "colored" together, as they don't blend well for some individuals. It's not uncommon for certain aspects to be amplified during hypnosis. Here, it was the intensity of brightness that became more pronounced.

Laura: It's still bright. I need some sunglasses!

I suggested to Laura that she was now sporting sunglasses. After a few seconds passed, Laura exclaimed, "It's still a bit bright!" My initial reaction was confusion—'What?!'—but then an idea popped into mind. Employing a touch of creativity, I suggested that she was now wearing sunglasses equipped with a special feature: automatic adjustment to any brightness level. If this solution didn't do the trick, I'm going home!

Laura: (starting to relax and smile) I see the butterfly. It's beautiful! It's green!
PM: Nice! And what is the butterfly doing now?
Laura: (enthusiastically) It's just flying!
PM: Isn't it amazing?
Laura: Yeah! I want to go with it!

PM: You can go with the butterfly for now... how do you feel?

Laura: It's so happy here!

PM: That's nice!

Laura: I want to stay...

"Bosconize" is a term I coined, which refers to the process of rendering someone's subconscious mind visible through hypnosis. This term was inspired by the name of the first visible subconscious form named Bosco.

Now that the test was a success, it's time to Bosconize Laura!

PM: ... you have an excellent imagination. And this is again the perfect time to use that amazing visualization or imagination to see your subconscious mind, Laura... describe it to me at the count of three. One... two... three!

Laura: I don't know... I can't open my eyes to see it.

PM: It's okay, you can leave your eyes closed.

Laura: (struggling hard to open her eyes but couldn't) I can't see it. I—I want to see it!

PM: It's okay, you can see it with your eyes closed. You can see it in your mind's eye. One, two, three— completely relaxed!

Your subconscious mind is part of you. It can sometimes show you pictures in your dreams. And it can show itself to you just like in a dream.

Allow your mind to relax. Allow your subconscious mind to form. To show itself to you in your mind's eye. And you can see it clearly, just like when you are dreaming, or imagining. And just allow your subconscious mind to reveal itself to you, at the count of three, clearly, even with your eyes closed. One... two... three.

Laura: I can almost see it, but...
(Speaking loudly and sounding excited) It's almost
there!

Making Laura's subconscious mind visible to her is proving
somewhat tricky. While bringing out Matt's subconscious form
was a breeze, and finding Liam's visible subconscious became
easier once he fully relaxed, Laura seemed to be encountering
ongoing difficulties in perceiving her subconscious mind's
form, as evident from her facial expression and body language.
Perhaps her desire to to see it was too intense. Nonetheless, I
persisted in probing her mind, seeking out what would work
best for her.

PM: How are you feeling?
Laura: I just can't tell.
PM: Any impressions coming to mind?
Laura: ... it looks like a reflection, and it just goes away.
PM: I understand. It seems like a fleeting reflection.
Laura: It wants to be there.
PM: Laura, allow your higher mind to speak through
you; let your subconscious guide you. Ask it how it can
reveal itself more clearly. And allow any impressions to
come to you. Let it give you the answer.
(A moment of silence as Laura searched for an answer)
And you can let me know the impressions or answers
that you get.
(After another pause without response) I'll count from
one to three again. When I reach three, you will come to
a time when you can visibly see your subconscious
mind freely, clearly, vividly, the way it wants you to see
it. One... two... three!
(A brief pause as I observe Laura's reaction) And it's
okay to use your imagination because your subcon-

scious mind is in charge of your imagination and your creativity. You are a creative woman, and your subconscious mind goes with you... what do you see?

After a brief pause, Laura's face lit up with a wide smile, signaling a breakthrough.

> **Laura:** I think it's the ocean.
> **PM:** You believe it's the ocean?
> **Laura:** It's the waves!
> **PM:** Waves?
> **Laura:** (excitedly) They're coming in!!!
> **PM:** Oh? How do you feel?
> **Laura:** I feel great! They're rolling in!!!
> **PM:** Woohoo! Exciting!
> **Laura:** And, now they're going back. They're going to go back!
> (Laura gasps and chuckles happily, then whispers) It's the waves!
> **PM:** The waves—is your subconscious mind the waves?
> **Laura:** I can't get to it, it comes in! And then it goes back!
> **PM:** How does it feel?
> **Laura:** (whispering) Feels so good!
> **PM:** Wonderful! And is it the representation of your subconscious mind?
> **Laura:** (Nods)
> **PM:** Right.
> **Laura:** Can I stay there?
> **PM:** Well, you can stay for a while, yes.
> (pausing to let her savor the experience) Is your subconscious mind communicating anything to you?
> **Laura:** Just no stress.
> **PM:** No stress to you—like how your subconscious mind has represented itself?

Laura: It's how I want to be.

PM: I see. Can you interact with it?

Laura: I can go with them when they're here.

PM: Go ahead.

Laura: And then they leave.

PM: Understood. The waves come and go, but your subconscious mind is with you. Although sometimes it may seem like it goes, it's actually with you. At the count of three, it's your subconscious mind's turn to come, and you will recognize it freely. One... two... three!

Describe what you see.

Laura: It's all around me.

PM: The waves?

Laura: Yeah, the water envelops me.

PM: Well, maybe your subconscious mind's form is the water... and you can always call on the water if you want...

Laura: (exhales audibly, appearing content)

PM: ... and your subconscious has the power to keep you calm. And just like the water, it can help you do a lot of things! It's versatile and full of potential. You just have to explore it, do you not?

Now, call on your subconscious. Ask the water, the waves, if it is your subconscious mind.

Laura: ...

PM: Any response?

Laura: It is!

PM: It is?

Laura: But, if I wanted it to be, it is!

PM: Excellent! Your visible subconscious has chosen the form that it wants to take for you. So that whenever you call on it, it will make you happy with its presence; to make its presence known to you. With that happy feeling it gives, by being able to help you, keep you company, and however you want it to be.

If it doesn't have a name, give it a name so you can call it anytime you want.

Laura: Joseph!

PM: Call on Joseph.

Laura: Joseph, please stay.

PM: What does Joseph say?

Laura: It wants to stay.

(As if speaking to someone present) Do you want me to stay?

PM: What does it say? (unsure whether to refer to it as "he" or "it")

Laura: Yes.

PM: That's good! Now, with your subconscious mind, anytime you want it to go, you can just tell it to go, and it will hide itself. However, it remains with you. Whenever you desire its presence or call upon "Joseph," your subconscious mind will appear before you.

Now, let's put that to the test. Tell Joseph to go away for now.

Laura: (hesitantly) I don't want Joseph to go away.

PM: Just for a brief moment. Tell Joseph to hide for now.

Laura: Okay. Go hide, Joseph.

PM: Let me know if Joseph is hiding.

Laura: ... He's not hiding. He's still here (smiling contentedly).

Okay, just for a minute...

Okay! Now he's gone!

PM: Now call on Joseph!

Laura: Joseph!

... I know, but you have to come back now.

... Okay.

PM: Is he back now?

Laura: Yup!

PM: Alright, that's good!

Laura: He doesn't want to go hide.

PM: Interesting! Now ask Joseph how he can assist you with your goals. Think of any goals you have right now and ask Joseph for his help. You can share his responses with me, too.

Laura: (addressing Joseph) So, you're going to wake me up to work out?

... Alright. Let's aim for losing 20 pounds by the end of the year.

... Okay. But you're going to wake me up early, though.

... Okay. We'll do it!

(chuckling) I know it's going to be tough!

... Okay.

PM: Okay?

Laura: (smiling, still engaged with Joseph) Yes.

PM: Are you finished asking Joseph about how he can support you with your goals?

Laura: (with a big smile) Yes!

PM: Perfect!

Laura: He's going to help me exercise. I'm going to lose 20 pounds this year!

PM: That's a fantastic goal!

Laura: Mm-hmm!

PM: Awesome! He'll keep you motivated!

Laura: Yes!

PM: Now, ask Joseph to sing a song.

Laura: ... Oh, my god, Joseph can't sing?... (covering her ears) Cover your ears... my god!

I couldn't contain my laughter upon hearing Laura's words and witnessing her joyful expression swiftly change to one of annoyance.

> **PM:** What is he singing?
> **Laura:** (throwing her hands up in the air and singing) God Bless America!!! Oh, my god!!!
> (pausing as if actually listening to something—or someone—then continues to sing) Land that the... that's not the right song! (bursting into laughter) Oh my god, Joseph... okay, stop!
> **PM:** Has he stopped now?
> **Laura:** Yeah, that was pretty awful! (chuckling)
> **PM:** Are you enjoying Joseph's company?
> **Laura:** Yeah!
> **PM:** Can you ask him if he can appear when you close your eyes and call on him?
> **Laura:** He says yes.
> **PM:** Okay, ask him if he can appear with your eyes open.
> **Laura:** ... He doesn't know... he thinks he can.
> **PM:** Alright, how about we test that? (I gave Laura further instructions before asking her to open her eyes.)
> **Laura:** (looking around) I don't see Joseph now.
> **PM:** Call him.
> **Laura:** Joseph?
> (long pause, her eyes darting around the room) I don't see Joseph.
> **PM:** It's okay. He'll come back.

I asked Laura to close her eyes and ensured she was deeply relaxed before resuming her exploration with Joseph.

> **PM:** Now call on Joseph.
> **Laura:** Joseph...

PM: Can you see Joseph?

Laura: ... Joseph's changing. He's like a teddy bear now! Aww...

PM: Do you like that?

Laura: I do! (smiling widely, she strokes the fur of an invisible teddy bear seemingly in front of her) You're so soft now!

PM: Maybe it's easier for you to see it if it's a teddy bear?

Laura: (continues caressing the fur of the invisible teddy bear) It's my surprise!

PM: Your surprise?

Laura: Yeah... I think he can be whatever I want him to be.
(having a conversation with Joseph) Are you for real? ... you can do that?

PM: What did he say?

Laura: He said he can be what I want it to be. He can be whatever I need him to be.

PM: Isn't that awesome?

Laura: (Enthusiastically) Yeah!

PM: And how would you like it if whenever you close your eyes anytime during the day, and you call on Joseph, you can see him vividly and clearly in your mind's eye, and you can talk to him, too?

Laura: Oh, yeah, that would be so fantastic!

PM: Sleep!

Laura reclined comfortably on the couch as I gently guided her back into a trance state. During this time, I offered her some final suggestions to consolidate her experience before wrapping up the session, ensuring that she would derive maximum benefit from it.

PM: Now that you've met Joseph, you've established a

visual connection to your subconscious mind. And isn't it incredible to interact with Joseph, knowing he can adapt to your needs and assist you with your goals? As your subconscious mind, he can influence both your mind and body positively.

From now on, even beyond this session, whenever you close your eyes and call on Joseph, he will appear instantly in your mind's eye. You can communicate with him freely because he is an integral part of you. With each interaction, Joseph will become more vivid and real to you, strengthening your connection and communication.

Joseph is not just a companion; he is also your mentor, guiding you through life's challenges. It's awesome, is it not? You will continue to interact with him even after this session, and with each passing day, your interactions will become clearer and more profound. Until maybe, one day, when you call on him, you may be pleasantly surprised to see Joseph with your eyes open, ready to engage with you.

So, at the count of five, you will return to your waking state, feeling relaxed, happy, and able to call on your subconscious mind anytime you want to.

One...

Two... feeling circulation returning, breathing shifting.

Three... very confident in your new discovery, your new friend, your subconscious mind, Joseph!

Four... starting to come back, and...

Five... open your eyes, wide awake, wide awake, wide awake! Welcome back!

Laura: (smiling warmly, eyes wide open) How did you do that?!

PM: (playfully) Magic! (I waved my hands in opposite circular motions, eliciting laughter.)

Laura: That was such a joyful experience!

I am pleased to have assisted Laura manifest her subconscious mind form, empowering her to achieve her goals more effectively through interacting with it. Now, my perfectionist nature has taken over. Before allowing her to leave, I wanted to ensure one final time she could still perceive Joseph in this highly awake state.

PM: How about you close your eyes now, and call on Joseph?
Laura: (closing her eyes) Joseph.
PM: (noticing Laura's lack of response and reaction for several seconds) Can you see him?
Laura: Yep! (After a brief pause, there was sudden excitement in her voice, and it seemed like the reality of Joseph started sinking in.) I can really see him!!!
PM: Awesome!
Laura: He almost looks human!!!
PM: Yeah, that's awesome, isn't it?
Laura: (opens her eyes, still in disbelief) Oh my god!
PM: You can interact with him—ask him questions, guidance, and all that.
Laura: It was always like that. But I didn't know it!
PM: Yeah. This is a new method that I developed. We always interact with our subconscious mind. It comes out when we're dreaming and all that. Or if we're in deep thought and suddenly the idea that we wanted pops up, that is the subconscious, and now it's easier to contact it.
Laura: Yeah! That was really good, Ponz! Why don't you do that for everybody?
PM: Yeah, that's why I am writing the book so that everybody may have it; it can help them!

Laura: Oh, wow... I feel renewed!

PM: That's awesome! You seem happier, too!

Laura: I wasn't happy when I first got here, but I feel so happy right now! (laughing hard) I literally was sitting on the truck crying because when I went to the bathroom, the guy in the grocery store was so mean. He told me there was no bathroom. I felt like he was being racist, and I don't like being treated like that.

PM: Maybe it's because of COVID. I went to a department store; they have a bathroom, but when I asked to use it, they said they don't have one because of COVID. And just as I was turning around, the lady said, "But if you really must, yes, we have a bathroom." I quickly replied, "Yeah, I have to!"

Laura: Yeah, I was feeling like not happy, and I feel so happy now!

PM: And you have your tool now—interactive Joseph.

Laura: Oh my god, I feel like a renewed spirit or something. Like I got something back!

PM: That's awesome!

Laura: Yeah, it's such a great feeling!

PM: I'm glad to be of help!

Laura: And, it's all free!!!

Thanks for not falling asleep on me, Laura! I might still hold you to that coffee next time! Helping Laura make her subconscious visible had its challenges, but it was an enlightening journey. At first, it felt like chasing a fleeting shadow in the dark, but encouraging her creativity and communication with her higher self seemed to help. Still, I couldn't shake the concern that her husband might call, worried about Laura's mental state, given her newfound experiences of conversing with someone only she could see and hear. However, I know he's open-minded and understanding.

Final Thoughts and Conclusion

In this chapter, we joined Laura, a vibrant woman in her fifties, as we explored the fascinating concept of making one's subconscious mind visible and interactive. Through Laura's experience, we gained insight into several fascinating aspects of the visible subconscious.

Key Insights

- **Elusiveness of the Subconscious:** Laura's initial encounter with her visible subconscious proved elusive, resembling a fleeting reflection. This highlights a challenge of accessing this hidden realm of the mind. However, once found, it remained with her.
- **Adaptive Nature:** Laura's subconscious, personified as Joseph, demonstrated adaptability, transforming from waves in an ocean to a teddy bear and even a human figure. This adaptability hints at the subconscious' ability to assume forms that resonate with an individual's needs and desires.
- **Interaction and Communication:** Laura's interactions with Joseph revealed that the visible subconscious can engage in conversations, offer guidance, and influence thoughts and actions. It serves as a mentor and a source of support, enriching one's inner dialogue.
- **Eyes-Closed Visualization:** Laura, like others, could only perceive her visible subconscious with her eyes closed. The reasons why some can see it with eyes open while others cannot remain unclear, warranting further exploration.

With that, you may wonder: what factors shape the appearance of a person's subconscious? What influences its behavior and responses? In the next chapter, we venture into the riveting account of an ex-military man who encounters his own eccentric subconscious, revealing valuable insights into these two aspects.

7

ETHAN'S DISCOVERY: CHARTING A PATH TO SUCCESS

 "Sometimes I've believed as many as six impossible things before breakfast."

— *LEWIS CARROLL*

E than, an amiable man in his early thirties, had transitioned from a military career to pursue further education due to an injury. Our conversation touched on the concept of the visible subconscious, which resonated deeply with Ethan's personal goals and challenges. Surprisingly, just two days later, he found himself comfortably seated in my hypnosis chair.

The transcript that follows recounts Ethan's session where his subconscious made its presence known. It reveals the unique form his subconscious took and the establishment of communication between Ethan and his visible subconscious (visub).

Without further ado, let's dive into the transcript of this remarkable conversation:

PM: At the count of three, you will see a friendly animal approach you. Describe it to me while remaining relaxed. One... two... three.

After a moment, I observed Ethan's eyeballs shifting behind his closed eyelids. This is a good sign!

Ethan: (smiling) I see an owl.
PM: As you see an owl, describe it to me further. What does it look like?
Ethan: Brown feathers, a white-gray face, big eyes, and a yellow-black beak.
PM: Okay. What is it doing now?
Ethan: Staring at me.
PM: Alright. Why do you think it is staring at you?
Ethan: Because I feel like that's what I'm doing with it! (laughing)
PM: Awesome! You have an excellent imagination, and this is helping you well. It is the perfect time to use that amazing visualization or imagination to see your subconscious mind.

I started leading Ethan through the process of visualizing his subconscious form, and we continued the session:

Ethan: ... I don't feel like I see anything at this point.
PM: That is totally fine. Just allow your mind to relax further and allow your mind to reveal your subconscious mind to you.
Now, I'm going to count from one to three. And when I reach three, I want you to move into a time when you can clearly, distinctly see your subconscious mind's form or shape. One... two... three.
Ethan: ...

PM: Do you see anything?
Ethan: (shaking his head) Uh-uh.

It seems Ethan might be in a state of deep relaxation where he can perceive things, but lacks the depth to fully see and engage with his subconscious. Another possibility is that his subconscious is elusive and hesitant to reveal itself. In order to facilitate a deeper state of hypnosis, I guided Ethan through a progressive body relaxation exercise. Following that, I conducted a brief test to assess his level of responsiveness.

> **PM:** At the count of three, you will see a hummingbird flying right in front of you. And you can describe it to me as you remain relaxed. One... two... three.
> **Ethan:** Bright green with see-through wings, a light belly, and a long, black mouth.
> **PM:** Can you see it clearly?
> **Ethan:** Yeah, it's hovering.
> **PM:** Now, at the count of three, you will immerse yourself in the experience with all your senses. One... two... three. Do you notice any changes?
> **Ethan:** The sound.
> **PM:** What about it?
> **Ethan:** I can hear a humming because of its fast wings!
> **PM:** Excellent! Now I want you to go and...
> (snapping my fingers) Sleep! Relax even more...

As Ethan settled more comfortably onto the couch, he assumed a disciplined posture, reminiscent of his military background. Inwardly, I quipped, "Well, soldier? Prepare to be Bosconized!" Recognizing Ethan's increased relaxation, I gently guided him towards tapping into his subconscious mind, pushing the boundaries a bit further. Despite Ethan's silence, subtle movements indicated progress, prompting me to offer further guidance.

> PM: Allow it to form, clearer and clearer, with every second that passes... until you see it fully, right in front of you.
>
> Ethan: ...
>
> PM: Coming to a point now where you can clearly see your visible subconscious at the count of three. One... two... three!

Ethan's face lit up with a delighted smile, sparking my curiosity about the source of his joy.

> PM: Describe what you see.
>
> Ethan: A Halloween pumpkin! (laughs)
>
> PM: Describe it further.
>
> Ethan: It's got slanted eyes, a jagged mouth, and it's glowing from within. Extremely orange and really healthy pumpkin!
>
> PM: And how does it make you feel?
>
> Ethan: Off! (laughs)
>
> PM: Can you interact with it?
>
> Ethan: No.
>
> PM: What is it doing now?
>
> Ethan: Sitting on some random porch, looking at me.
>
> PM: Ask it if it's your subconscious mind.
>
> Ethan: ... I'm not getting a response.
>
> PM: That's okay. At the count of three, your subconscious mind will feel safer and more confident to talk to you, using gestures, words, sounds, anything it can to communicate with you. One... two... three! Now ask it again if it's your subconscious mind.
>
> Ethan: The light flickers.

PM: Which light?

Ethan: Inside the pumpkin.

PM: How many times did it flicker?

Ethan: Non-stop.

PM: Ask if the flashing light means yes.

Ethan: ... I think so.

PM: Okay, now ask it to communicate the meaning of "No."

Ethan: ... I see the porch but from a different angle.

PM: Describe that angle.

Ethan: Where I couldn't see the face with the pumpkin, but I could see basically the entire patio. It's like an old, white house with some of the wood visible through the panes. There are old columns and a black screen door.

PM: Okay. What did you ask before it shifted to this view?

Ethan: I asked, "Subconscious, will you show me what 'no' means?" Then it created that image.

PM: So, when you see that view, it means "no." When the light is continuously flickering, it means "yes." Now, ask if it has a name.

Ethan: ... No response.

PM: Alight. Let's try this. (snapping my fingers) Sleep! At the count of three, I want you to relax even more. Deeper than your deepest sleep ever! One... two... three! Once more, use your imagination or visualization fully. I'm going to count from one to three, and when I reach three, that will be the point where you can see your subconscious mind, or the representation of your subconscious mind, and you can interact with it. One... two... three!

Ethan: ... Oh, I see a river now.

PM: You see a river! Describe it more.

Ethan: The water's opaque. The flow seems fast but

restricted. Thick, green grass three to five feet tall lines both banks.

PM: How does it make you feel seeing that river?

Ethan: Like home.

PM: Feels like home. Alright, ask if it's the representation of your subconscious mind.

Ethan: ... I don't feel any change.

PM: Ask it to change into a form you can communicate with easily.

Ethan: Okay, I don't know if that's just me, but I see... a human, but made of water!

PM: A human in water form, right in front of you?

Ethan: Yes.

PM: Can you describe it more?

Ethan: She's extremely blue, transparent, with long hair, and has the perfect outline of the human body.

PM: Alright. Ask if it's your subconscious.

Ethan: I got a big head nod!

PM: That's a yes! Perfect! Ask for its name.

Ethan: ... nothing.

PM: Give it a name.

Ethan: Umm... Blue! (smiles really nicely)

PM: Blue, okay. Now, think of a goal. Something simple.

Ethan: Beat my classmate in an endurance run?

PM: Alright, ask Blue to help you achieve that.

Ethan: Okay...

PM: What did she say?

Ethan: Head nods and a goofy little smirk! Like when you're super happy, and you nod super fast.

PM: Very positive then! Now, think of another easy goal.

Ethan: Work out consistently.

PM: What challenge are you encountering?

Ethan: Discipline.

PM: Okay, ask Blue how she can help with discipline.

Ethan: She just stares back, like you know the answer kind of thing.

PM: What did you ask specifically?

Ethan: I asked, "Blue, how can you help me work out more consistently?" And I got the blank stare back like, "You answered your own question."

PM: Okay, is there anything specific that you want Blue to help you with?

Ethan: Help me be more motivated internally.

PM: Now ask Blue to make it so that you are very motivated every time you do your workout.

Ethan: ... I got a head nod!

PM: There you go! It looks like Blue, your official (visible) subconscious, will help you be or feel more motivated to work out. That's good!

Ethan: Blue's rough! (laughs briefly)

PM: How about asking Blue to sing a song?

Ethan: ... She just planted a song in my head! "Meet Me at Her Spot" by Willow Smith. It just went straight to that song, and it's now stuck in my head!

PM: Is she singing it?

Ethan: It went into the actual song, rather.

PM: How so? Can you hear the lyrics clearly?

Ethan: Oh yeah. I can hear the music, the words, everything.

PM: So, Blue played that song for you when you asked her to sing. Is that correct?

Ethan: Yeah, because I wasn't even thinking about that song before she brought it up.

PM: Alright. Now, you're learning more about how Blue communicates with you.

Ethan: It makes sense because the song relates to someone who's a really high motivator for me.

PM: That's great! Looks like Blue's already making a difference.

Ethan: Yeah, it's a positive sign.

PM: Yeah. Aren't you glad you met Blue?

Ethan: Goddamn it, Blue. (laughs)

PM: Ask Blue if she can also communicate via words or sounds.

Ethan: ... With words, immediate no. With sounds, it's a circle nod that's like "I think so."

PM: And how does she indicate "No"?

Ethan: Like this! (imitates a cheek flip and chuckles)

PM: Alright, those are her indications for yes and no. It's good to have that clarity. Now, Ethan, having met Blue, you've established a visual connection with your subconscious mind. And isn't it amazing to engage with Blue, knowing that she can embody whatever you need her to be? You can enlist her help in achieving your goals because she is your subconscious mind. She holds the power to influence your thoughts and actions, guiding both your mind and body. From this point forward, and even beyond this session, whenever you require Blue's presence, simply call her name, "Blue," and instantly, her image will materialize in your mind's eye or even before you with your eyes open. You can interact with her freely because she is an integral part of you. Even after this session, you can continue to engage with her. Your interaction will evolve and become more vivid with each passing day. It's truly an incredible and empowering experience, is it not?

I decided to briefly bring Ethan out of hypnosis to gather his thoughts on the experience thus far.

Ethan: (smiling after opening his eyes) It's weird! At

times, it feels like I'm almost steering the experience, yet there are moments when things unfold beyond my conscious control. For instance, when you asked about Blue's meaning for 'No,' the image of her moving her head flashed in my mind even before I asked the question.

PM: That's great because she's deeply connected to you. She picks up on what you perceive and responds promptly.

Ethan: Yeah, it's uncanny! Whenever she nods, it's as if I'm zooming in on her face, and seeing what's almost like a happy yes.

PM: Alright. Sometimes you won't need to see her. So, when you wish to temporarily dismiss her presence, simply say, "Blue, go hide," or express gratitude with "Thank you, Blue," or bid her farewell with "I'll see you later." She'll fade from view but remain within you. Whenever you need her assistance, just summon her, and she'll be there, always eager to support you because she's genuinely invested in your well-being.

Ethan: I like this Blue!

PM: Are you enjoying her presence?

Ethan: Absolutely.

PM: (I looked at him, smiled, raised my hand, and snapped my fingers) Sleep!

As Ethan closed his eyes and relaxed into a comfortable position on the couch, adopting his familiar soldier-like stance, I proceeded with the hypnosis session by presenting him with positive affirmations. While I was keen to gauge his perception of Blue with his eyes open, discussing his overall experience remained equally essential. Nevertheless, I couldn't help but be intrigued by this particular aspect of his session.

PM: I'll count from one to five, and when I reach five, I want you to open your eyes. Blue will appear vividly before you, engaging all your senses. One... two... three... four... five!

Ethan: (Opening his eyes, then looking ahead and slightly to his left. He seems to focus on something invisible to me, scanning from head to foot.) Blue's taller than I thought! (chuckles)

PM: Taller? Can you describe her?

Ethan: Yeah!

PM: Where is she?

Ethan: Right here. (He stands up, walks a few steps forward, then pauses. He gazes upward as if addressing a taller figure. He stretches his hand up and places it atop Blue's head.) And about... good god!

PM: Taller than you?

Ethan: Definitely!

PM: Does she still resemble water?

Ethan: Oh, a clear blue, like water! A very nice figure. Her hair is exceptionally long, also blue but with a distinct clarity, almost like Cinderella's glass slipper. And... she has a belly button now!

PM: A belly button?

Ethan: (laughing) She didn't have one before, but she does now! (studying the figure) That's weird!

PM: Alright, ask her to temporarily go away.

Ethan: ... Alright.

PM: Is she gone?

Ethan: Yes.

PM: Now, call her back.

Ethan: That was quick!

PM: She's here?

Ethan: Yeah. Lightning fast! Like the superhero Flash, she swooshes in! (gesturing from behind him to the left, then swinging his hand forward) But in a watery form, appearing just here!

PM: Impressive!

Ethan: But a bit farther back this time, near the couch.

PM: Like approximately how far? About six feet away?

Ethan: Yes, roughly.

PM: Fascinating!

Ethan: I find it much easier to see her that way! (laughs)

PM: Alright, let's conduct a few experiments. Is that Fanta Orange? (Referring to the canned drink on the couch's holder.)

Ethan: Yes.

PM: Ask Blue to change its taste to... grape! See what she says.

Ethan: ... She's giving me this look like, "Really? You want me to do what?"

PM: Say something like, "Blue, make it so that this Fanta tastes like grape."

Ethan: (glancing at Blue) Alright, here goes.

PM: What's her response?

Ethan: She did this little gesture of like, "Fine, I'll do it!" You know, like a fairy godmother granting a wish. Like, "Bonk! There you go!" Let's see. (takes a sip and pauses, inspecting the can) Definitely tastes different!

PM: How different?

Ethan: It's lost the intense orange flavor, now it's more like a subtle grape taste.

PM: So, the taste changed?

Ethan: Slightly, yes.

PM: Isn't that interesting?

Ethan: I want my orange back! (laughs, takes two gulps, then laughs again, almost spitting out the drink) That's bizarre!

PM: What happened?

Ethan: It's definitely orange now!

PM: And when you requested her to change it back, what was her response?

Ethan: Oh, she was like, "Okay," with a happy face. And I was like, "Okay, give me my orange!" And just like that, it was orange again.

PM: Impressive! Now, how about we conduct a pain test?

Ethan: A what?

PM: A brief pain test!

Ethan: (hesitates slightly) Okay.

Ethan's response caught me off guard, revealing a subtle concern in his demeanor. It was unexpected, especially considering his military background. Perhaps my expectations were too high. Nonetheless, Ethan's willingness to participate demonstrated commendable sportsmanship.

At this point in the session, I aimed to test whether this water figure possessed some of the capabilities exhibited by other visible subconscious forms and to observe how it would respond to various requests. Let's find out!

PM: Let me see. What do I have here? I have nothing to poke you with... (rummaging through the cabinet) Ah, here we go! A toothpick!

Ethan: How do you want to do it?

PM: We'll use your arm. Your right arm—right in the middle.

Ethan: (extends his right arm, palm up)

PM: I'm going to poke it (proceeds to poke the middle area of the arm a few times). Can you feel it?

Ethan: Just a little bit.

PM: Yeah, just some slight pokes, so you can feel it.

Ethan: Yeah!

PM: Several pokes... okay. Now ask Blue to make this part of your arm numb (draws a circle of a small area with the index finger).

Ethan: Okay.

PM: Yeah, so you won't feel any pain.

Ethan: It's like I barely had to ask her. She just tells me, "It's okay, I got you."

PM: Okay. (starts poking different areas of the arm) Can you feel it?

Ethan: A little. That first one was really numb.

PM: Alright. (continues to poke a few more areas on the arm)

Ethan: It's like, if you go around here, it's way numb. It's like in certain areas, there's a loss of feeling, but not everywhere.

PM: I see. Which part?

Ethan: In certain areas along this one (points to some areas on his arm with his finger) there's one or two I felt over here. But then I didn't feel like two or three around... I think it was in this area.

PM: Uh-hum. Maybe it's because I drew the area with my finger earlier. But when I poked outside of that, you were feeling it. I'll poke it again inside. (pokes twice) Can you feel it?

Ethan: It's so barely, though.

PM: So, it's numb.

Ethan: Sorry, I can barely... I can feel a little bit.

PM: Sorry, you have so many pokes already. So, you have the sensation of something poking but no pain?

Ethan: Whenever you did the first ones, they were almost like little pinches. But this one, it's just kind of digging in, it's like, of course, I can feel something pushing on my skin, if that makes sense.

PM: Alright. That's good! So, it's working. Ask her to make it normal.

Ethan: It's almost like seeing her in my head's almost better!

PM: Oh, when you close your eyes?

Ethan: Well, not even close my eyes. I could just stare and, like, I see her next to that river, like that scenario.

PM: Okay. How about closing your eyes and calling on Blue.

Ethan: Uh-hum.

PM: Can you see her?

Ethan: Yeah! I can see her with my eyes open, too.

PM: So, it's both when you have your eyes open and close. Is it clear when you have your eyes closed, like she's over there?

Ethan: She is a lot closer when my eyes are closed. But it's when my eyes are open that she's a little further.

PM: Okay. So, what do you think about the experience?

Ethan: Oh, it was kind of weird! At first, I was a bit anxious, like, "It's not coming to me!" Then when you mentioned counting down for an animal to appear, a wolf immediately came to me, so I thought, "Well, I already know what this animal's going to be." But right when you hit "three," an owl comes out of nowhere! I was like, "WTF is this? What just happened?" And then there was this moment where I'm staring at this picture frame, and suddenly, there's this owl right there, looking left at me. I'm like, "Why am I seeing a freaking owl!?" (laughs) That definitely threw me off! But it just kept staring at me without moving. I was like, "Um, okay." And then, bam, the river appeared out of nowhere. It was the first image that really came to life. But it didn't do anything until you said to communicate differently. Then it was like, "Okay, here's your water figure!" Or water... I don't even know what to call it... Blue! I definitely need to come up with a better name for Blue.

But yeah, it was weird because I wasn't used to asking questions like that. I was like, "Let me ask the question first." But Blue was just like, "Uh-hum, uh-hum, whatever..." you know? Like a nod for yes, the half-ass gesture (moves his head in a circular motion), and there was like the "Fine, but I don't want to do it."

PM: When you say "I don't want to do it," how do you mean?

Ethan: It's like when you ask someone to do something and they agree reluctantly but with a playful attitude. You know, that kind of goofy face, like a playful "Fiiiiine!" when they want to tease you. Just like when she changed the drink flavor. It definitely had that vibe!

And I didn't feel like I was controlling anything. Whenever I answered my own questions, it felt like my subconscious speaking. Because my subconscious isn't going to be like, "Okay, here you go. Figure it out," you know?

So that was kind of cool. I expected it to be like, "Now, here, x, y, and z, go and do this, not that..." you know. It sounds like my subconscious, especially with that look on her face. It was just like, "Really? Do you want me to give you the answer when you already know? You just want to repeat yourself again?"

With discipline and everything, I sometimes ask myself, "I know the answer to that question." So now, whenever I ask her for help, it's like, "Okay, help me with... like that internal motivation, and make it so I want to go every time," pretty much. That's when it went finally like, okay, there's something different. Like, "Okay. Yes, that's fine." So, it's almost like it challenges me as well to think critically, not just be like, "Look, give me yes or no."

PM: That's good! Before I ask you any more questions, I have to run to the restroom really quick.

Ethan: Oh, yeah, go for it! I'm going to stand up real quick.

PM: I'll be back! Just have a conversation with Blue!

After a brief two-minute break...

PM: Okay, is there anything else you think you need help with? For some people, it's about motivation, waking up...

Ethan: I think the motivation part will help a bit, now that Blue and I have met.

PM: (noticing Ethan's romantic tone) Uh-hum.

Ethan: And I think I can have more specific goals with alcohol and nicotine. I think that would be a good starting point to ask. Like, I just need to have a little conversation. And it's like, "Look, there are just some things in life that I want to keep changing. Just help me keep moving that way" kind of thing.

PM: And what did she say?

Ethan: Yeah, she nodded!

PM: The happy nod.

Ethan: Right. It's more like, "Okay, you're acknowledging that I am your subconscious, and you can't fool me!" (laughs) My bad, sorry. I was trying to take the easy way, I know. But yeah, I think that was pretty much how that went. Because I think those are the main things. Working out pretty much got my life back on track to where I wanted to go. Like, I need to work on specifics because I kind of feel like Blue is harping on me for a second there about that. So, I got to be better about that.

And I think when I have very specific statements that are stronger, it's a lot easier for her to be like, "Yes" or "No." It can't be more generalized statements. Otherwise, I get the look!

PM: Yeah! The statement that usually works is, for example, "Blue, make it so that I am motivated..." In the present tense—"I am motivated every time to do my workout." Something like that.

Ethan: So, present tense and specific.

PM: Yeah.

Ethan: Okay. Ha! I get it! It's kind of like having your own little genie!

PM: Yes, exactly!

Ethan: And she's pretty good-looking, too! (laughs) Apparently, I have a thing for hot wom... yeah! Apparently!

PM: (nodding) Even with your subconscious.

Ethan: Yeah, I know! What the hell?!

PM: Yeah, because that form's acceptable to you, remember?

Ethan: Yeah! Choose a form that I can, right? And um, so that goddamn song... oh my god, now I have to show you. And I bet you've heard it, too. Let me see. (Taking out his mobile phone, searching for the song online, and playing it. The slow beat of the cymbals fills the small room, and after a few seconds, a female voice sings about waking up but having trouble doing so; having slept through the day, and realizing she wasn't getting any younger.) Have you ever heard this song?

PM: No, I haven't.

Ethan: So, the lyrics in it literally remind me of someone. It's talking about two people who care about each other and catch a vibe. About wanting to stay home for the night after looking into the person's eyes. Then it's talking about the guy who says that he got a drunk text, which we've done, and then it's telling the other person to meet at their spot. And pretty much, we have our own spot where we go to, where we'd go for walks or just sit and chat.

And it's kind of funny. The song has been on my mind like crazy lately. And so, it's kind of funny that Blue plays that song.

PM: So, it's timely!

Ethan: Right!

PM: You mentioned nicotine and drinking. What is your specific goal about that?

Ethan: I don't know yet. That's what I need to work on.

PM: Alright.

Ethan: Because I enjoy it. And so, I like to keep telling myself, "You need to quit before you graduate from school." Well, at the same time, I know half of me is like, "Do you really want to do that? Do you REALLY want to do that? Because I know you!" So, I don't know. I definitely want to calm down and, like, not smoke anywhere near as much, that's for sure!

PM: Okay, so reducing it.

Ethan: Big time!

PM: Reducing it from what to what? How many sticks do you smoke in a day?

Ethan: About a pack a day. Well, I never smoke a pack. But, let's say right around fifteen a day.

PM: And mostly, you did that smoking before because you were bored, or...

Ethan: Right. Habit, coping... many reasons—because I ate, because I had sex, because I went for a jog, because I worked out, it's like every time I go to my car. There are so many habits, so I need to break those. I don't need to smoke literally after everything, but I do!

PM: Yeah, that's a wonderful goal! And so, what other reasons do you think you should consider for stopping smoking?

Ethan: Oh. For my job.

PM: For your job?

Ethan: Yeah! Absolutely! I mean, nobody wants to get massaged by somebody who smokes. Nobody also wants to see a personal trainer who smokes. I think, in both career fields, it would be nice to quit. Or where it's like I only smoke one or maybe less than five a day, or something like that.

PM: Less than five sticks a day, and not when you're doing your work. Perhaps after your work or something.

Ethan: Yeah, that would be nice.

PM: That's a good goal. Would you like to talk to Blue about that one? See how she helps you with that? And tell her when you want to smoke those—if it's in the evening, etc.

Ethan: Oh, I got to think more about that before I ask.

PM: Okay. Or maybe you can ask her to make it so that you reduce your smoking to half a pack? You can try that and see how she helps you with it.

Ethan: ... it's like she's kind of saying yes, but at the same time, almost not. Like a yes and no answer?

PM: (winking) Ask her to remove that habit.

Ethan: She straight up said, "No" on that one! (laughing) Remind me how I should word these again.

PM: "Blue, make it so that I am smoking half a pack a day..." kind of reason out. "Because I want to be healthy," or something.

Ethan: Okay. Blue, make it so that I only smoke half a pack a day, nothing more, or... kind of like that?

PM: Yeah! "...because I have no need to smoke for more..."

Ethan: ... Okay. Alright. I asked to make it so that I smoke way less per day unless I am socially smoking. And then I got the nice head nod.

PM: Perfect! Starting tonight or tomorrow, let me know the changes that you notice.

Ethan: Okay. Yeah, of course!

PM: How about the drinking?

Ethan: The drinking? Let's see. Hmmm...

PM: What level are you at now?

Ethan: On a moderate level. It's not too bad. Like this week, I've just been drinking more. Well, it's party central this week. But before that, it's like, you know, I've been taking days intermittently. But I think I want to take at least three days off minimum in a row. Not every day, because it's supposed to be great for your liver if you take at least three days in a row off. I don't want it to be like, one day here, one day there, or two days there. I want to make sure I do at least three days in a row throughout the week. So, Blue. Make it so... (chuckling a little) ...that I take off three days per week from drinking. Blue! Get over here!

PM: Is she a bit far?

Ethan: Yeah... okay, I got a nice smile.

PM: Awesome! Let me know also what she says.

Ethan: She didn't say anything. It's like I'm kind of in my own brain right now, just trying to wrap around how I can stare and ask a question. It's almost like I don't want to be the person who gives me that response. Where it's like, "Oh, no, I did that," you know? Does it make sense? So, I'll sit there and stare at Blue, like, "You are now to answer this. Otherwise, I will not believe you." You know, something like that.

PM: Is it something like a doubt?

Ethan: Right! And so, it's kind of funny how something

different, like, how that smile just kind of happens where it was different. But not like, okay, hey, I'm just really seeing the head nod over and over. It was like, okay, here's a nicer way to answer that question. So, it's kind of like, boom! Mind-blowing almost to a point. Like, it's weird how it works!

PM: Yeah. It's something new.

Ethan: Yeah!

PM: You've got a new friend!

Ethan: Right?! Shit! I'm going to tell my friends, "I'm going on a date tonight, and you don't even know!" (laughing) Oh, shit!

So, it's 8 o'clock. I forgot I was picking up my great-aunt. She has an appointment at 10:30 tomorrow, and I have an appointment at 10 o'clock—which I just made the other day because I completely forgot about my aunt. I need to call them in the morning and see if I can come in a little bit early. Or I can just drop my aunt off really early and I'll just pick her up.

PM: Alright. So, sit back, and we'll do some finishing touches.

Ethan: Okay!

PM: I need you to close your eyes and (snapping my fingers) sleep!

Concluding the hypnosis session, I provided Ethan additional positive reinforcements and gently guided him out of the trance state once again.

Ethan: I definitely feel relaxed!

PM: That's good! Aren't you glad you came here?

Ethan: Yes, I am! I'm glad that you actually offered and did that; I appreciate it! It turned out fucking great! Nothing was what I expected! Nothing like... I don't know. I didn't really have any expectations, I guess. And I was like, "Well, let's just see what happens!" Man, I feel like I just met a hot new friend! That blows my mind! Alright, cool! Good job, subconscious!

PM: So, your homework, as part of this, is to give me updates when you discover something or if she does something. Like, if you ask her to do something and you discover what she can do, let me know.

Ethan: Okay!

PM: So, utilize her in whatever way you can! Her response is quick, too, just like with the toothpick earlier.

Ethan: That was weird because half of my arm was numb, and the other half kind of wasn't.

PM: Yeah. Also, with pain. If you have pain—stub your toe or something—ask her to make it so that the pain is one instead of ten or something.

Ethan: I did that, actually. When I was sitting, my right knee started cramping up and hurt really bad. So, when I got up, I was like, "Hey, Blue, fix this!" So yeah, it doesn't feel crappy anymore.

PM: How fast did it take?

Ethan: So, whenever I got up the first time, it was cramping, and then Blue just nods; it's not hurting now. And that's why I was like, "Oh, hey, by the way..." That's when I just literally noticed it. How cool, my knee doesn't hurt!

PM: You noticed the change pretty quickly once you asked her.

Ethan: Yeah. That was interesting. Hmmm... it makes me think, that's for sure!

PM: She can control your bodily functions, just like the subconscious.

Ethan: Well, it's like, really, the power of the mind. It's so hard to grasp it because it's so new, I guess, you know? Man, I wish I had a class tomorrow! I want to tell everybody!

PM: Okay, but don't tell the therapist you're seeing about that one. Because they might think you're schizophrenic.

Ethan: Oh! (bursts out laughing)

PM: Uh-huh. Just a warning!

Ethan: If I explain it how, it's like, "Oh hey, it came just like how you visualize a person right in front of you as if you could see the person right in front of you..." I think I can word it something like that.

PM: Or you can also explain it and just tell them you went to a registered Clinical Hypnotherapist here in Washington. Tell them it's a new technique for contacting your subconscious.

———

THE FOLLOWING DAY, ETHAN CONTACTED ME, EAGER TO EXPLORE further into his visible subconscious. We set up a brief check-in session for late afternoon.

Ethan: Whenever I envision that spot, it looks like she's sort of with the river. And so, there's the river, right? When she emerged from the river, it was as if there was a cord that linked her to it. But it's like a cord made of water. It maintains its form without splashing anywhere — it just stays intact. It flows out of the river, runs across the grass, and then connects to her. Yeah!

Today, I first noticed the cord because it was behaving almost like a towel earlier. It intrigued me, and then I realized, "Oh, that's the connection to the river! I get it! Gotcha!"

PM: So, that river is maybe your main subconscious mind, and she's connected to that. She's the representation of it.

Ethan: Right. Because when we asked, "Hey, we need somebody to communicate with," that's how she just emerged. It was through those cord-like... I don't even know.

PM: Okay. What other conversations did you have with her?

Ethan: It was definitely about staying focused.

PM: How did you ask her?

Ethan: I just brought it up. I was like, "Hey, I really need help staying focused today. Will you help me with that?" That's pretty much how I asked. And I think it's word for word like that.

PM: Yeah, asking for help. That also works. Also, be positive in stating what you want.

Ethan: I think my subconscious was like, "Oh yeah." Yup, you heard me. At least I have Blue now. The woman of my dreams! I have yet to actually have her speak to me.

PM: Words?

Ethan: Yeah. Still no words.

PM: Hmmm... when we had the hypnosis, I asked you to ask it if it can speak in words, and it said no. Right? So, it doesn't want to communicate in words. But for some people, it's sometimes a mixture. And for others, it's just words, so they can hear the words being spoken by that subconscious. I guess it's a bit different.

Ethan: Weird how it works like that, though.

PM: (jokingly) Maybe it's because you'll bug it a lot more once it talks to you.

Ethan: Uh-huh. Probably.

PM: Ask it to tell you why it doesn't want to communicate in words.

Ethan: If I ask that way, do you think it would even answer because it already does not?

PM: I don't know. You can always try.

Ethan: (looking directly in front of him) I'm kind of just getting a blank stare.

PM: So, it really doesn't want to.

Ethan: No.

PM: The other person who could see it used to talk to him in his own voice, but sounded more confident. And it stopped doing that. Now, it responds with beeps and gestures. But if there's a question that requires a more complicated answer, it inserts it in his mind. So, he asks, and then the thoughts that come into his mind are the answers, and he knows it is. So, it's very different.

Ethan: Oh. Maybe it's saying something about the person's subconscious. Like, maybe it's because I can really be reserved sometimes, so I wonder if it plays into that or something, you know?

PM: (jokingly) You? Reserved?

Well, the subconscious representation reflects some of the personality of the person who has it. That's what I noticed.

Ethan: I totally can see it. It also makes sense that she's a really hot lady. Because, like, yeah, you are so my subconscious right there. You knew me! Way too well! I will pay attention to you!

PM: I was wondering about that. Because I know you're a well-spoken man. Very goofy. And your subconscious is... a bit quiet. It doesn't want to talk. So, I was wondering about that yesterday. I was like, "Why?"

Ethan: Most of the time, I'm pretty reserved. Like, for this part, I do plenty of observing and a lot of listening.

For the most part, I would rather just watch and listen then base my actions on what is happening.

PM: Okay. That explains it!

Ethan: Even when I'm at home. I'm not a big talker at all with Mom. I'd rather just sit outside with my dogs.

PM: How come? What's different?

Ethan: I'd rather talk to friends. With my mom, I see her all the time. I don't need to talk to them all the time. Like, "I talked enough today. I'm done." Like, "Call your sister." You know? All the time, it's just the type of talking that happens. It's just so different from my normal that I'm just like, "Uh..." I love her to death, but still. Damn.

Usually, she'll want to tell me about her whole day. Tell me about every little detail. It is nice, though, sometimes having that company. But other times, I go in the backyard if it's nice out. And I will chill for the rest of the night out there.

Oh, by the way, I noticed Blue looks a little different.

PM: What differences did you notice?

Ethan: I noticed that there were little petals everywhere throughout her hair. Her hair didn't change color, nothing like that. It's just the accessories that changed. And so, in her hair, near the intersection, I noticed she just had a bunch of flower petals all throughout. And so sometimes I check, and her hair definitely changes! That makes a lot of sense, too. Because one thing I will always tell a girl is, "I want to know how you take care of your hair. I like your hair." It's so funny!

And that is why, whenever I was talking to the girl I liked, I was asking her, "So what things are you really meticulous about? I have a feeling about one."

And she's like, "So I'm kind of bougie about my hair." I'm like, "I knew it. I knew it!" That hair. Dude! If you could fall in love with hair, that would be it! She put the juju on me with that. Fuck! I'm so fucked!

Towards the end of 2023, I purchased a copy of *The Silva Mind Control Method*. In this book, Silva and Miele (1989) recounted the experience of a graduate of the Mind Control course who encountered an elderly mute woman during their meditative practice. This woman communicated using yes and no nods and limited sign language, serving as a counselor for the graduate. [1] In this context, a counselor was not a physical being but rather a representation of the individual's subconscious or higher self. They provided guidance, wisdom, and assistance whenever the individual entered a meditative state.

Interestingly, this counselor bears some resemblance to Ethan's visible subconscious mentor named Blue. However, Blue is much quicker to contact for Ethan. This observation raises the intriguing possibility that both figures may be tapping into the same underlying aspect of the individuals' psyches, accessed through different representations or pathways.

Final Thoughts and Conclusion

In this chapter, we've delved deep into the fascinating world of the visible subconscious, uncovering the remarkable capabilities and unique characteristics of these inner companions. From Ethan's encounter with his own visible subconscious, Blue, to the insights gained about how they operate, we've witnessed the potential for transformative experiences within ourselves.

Key Insights

- **Unique Personal Representations:** Visible subconscious forms vary widely, reflecting individual personality traits, preferences, and even quirks.
- **Non-Verbal Communication:** Some of these inner companions communicate through gestures, facial expressions, and body movements rather than words, providing insight into the subtleties of our subconscious minds. They also sometimes answer even before the person finishes asking, as if they can expect one's thoughts.
- **Manipulating Sensations:** Visible subconscious forms can alter perceptions, changing the taste and scent of items, numbing sensations, and easing physical discomfort.
- **Motivation and Focus:** Using their presence for guidance and support, individuals can enhance their motivation and maintain focus on specific goals.
- **Personal Growth:** Engaging with your visible subconscious can lead to self-discovery, greater self-awareness, and personal growth.

As you continue to explore and engage with the visible subconscious, remember that this inner companion can serve as a powerful ally on the journey of self-discovery and personal development. Harnessing its unique abilities and understanding its non-verbal cues can unlock opportunities for profound experiences and meaningful transformation.

In the following chapter, dive into an interview with a visible subconscious. Discover its capabilities and become enlightened as it unveils the key to harnessing its power—direct from the source!

8

GLIMPSE BEHIND THE VEIL: INTERVIEW WITH A VISIBLE SUBCONSCIOUS

 "Depend more upon the intuitive forces from within and not harken so much to that of outside influences— but learn to listen to that still small voice from within."

— EDGAR CAYCE

As I ventured into the realm of visible subconscious (visub) forms, a multitude of revelations emerged from my interactions with various individuals. One striking observation that recurred frequently was the profound influence of the language used by the requester when engaging with their visub. This observation underscores a fundamental principle governing the elicitation of favorable responses from the subconscious mind, hinting at a universal guideline for effective communication with it.

Among the questions that surfaced repeatedly during these interactions, two stood out. The first inquiry centered on the extent of the visub's capabilities, prompting individuals to consider the full range of tasks it could undertake. The second query revolved around the most effective approach to formulating requests that would optimize the visub's willingness to provide assistance.

To address these inquiries, I devised a plan to consult the visible subconscious itself. If there were an equivalent of a teacher's pet in the realm of visible subconscious forms, it would undoubtedly be Bosco.

On July 31, 2022, I scheduled Matt, one of my participants, for a brief hypnosis session. The transcript below encapsulates the enlightening dialogue that unfolded with Bosco while Matt was in a trance.

> **PM:** Matt, I want you to call on Bosco.
> **Matt:** Bosco!
> **PM:** Bosco can act as our translator and communicate with you as needed. Ask Bosco how you can better communicate with him regarding your goals.
> **Matt:** (directed at Bosco) How can I communicate better with you regarding my goals?
> ... he says you just be direct.
> **PM:** Okay, can he provide an example of how you should ask him?
> **Matt:** (directed at Bosco) Can you give me an example of how to ask you stuff?
> ... Bosco reiterates the need to be direct and specific.
> **PM:** Ask Bosco how else he can help you with your goals and what else he can do for you.
> **Matt:** (directed at Bosco) What else can you do for me?
> ... Bosco says he can help channel focus and surface traits and abilities that I already have.

Bosco's claim to channel focus and unearth hidden talents resonates with the belief that many harbor untapped potential.

Instances of individuals suddenly gaining fluency in a new language or developing musical prowess later in life without formal training underscore this possibility. There are also recorded cases of hyperthymesia, a rare condition marked by an exceptional autobiographical memory, where individuals can recall detailed events from their past with remarkable clarity and accuracy. In addition, there are instances of acquired savant syndrome, where people demonstrate sudden and exceptional abilities in fields like mathematics, music, and art. While I haven't explored this aspect of the visible subconscious yet, I can't help but envision the possibility for more people to unlock their hidden talents, a process that could prove transformative and enriching.

PM: What else can he do?

Matt: (directed at Bosco) What else?

... he can help me remember things... he can help me think logically... reduce stress and keep me calm.

PM: Anything else?

Matt: (directed at Bosco) Uh... what else can you do?

... Bosco says he can do lots of things. He says I can ask him anything, and he can see if he can help.

PM: What can he do with the body?

Matt: He can help me heal faster. He can take away the pain or dull pain. He can calm me down...

PM: Can he help with motion sickness?

Matt: ... Yes.

PM: Can he communicate with someone else's subconscious mind?

Matt: No, he can only communicate with me.

PM: Can two visible subconscious minds communicate with each other with both people's approval?

Matt: He says he can only see me.

PM: Ask him if he is your subconscious or if he is the unconscious as well.

Matt: (directed at Bosco) Are you my subconscious or unconscious?

... Bosco says he's me.

I probably could have skipped the last question since it delves into specific terminology, but it's still valuable to have received an answer from Bosco. Essentially, the subconscious subtly shapes our thoughts and behaviors without our awareness, while the unconscious encompasses deeper layers of our mind, including hidden memories and instincts. Though people often interchange these terms in everyday language, they hold distinct meanings in psychology.

PM: Can he show you visions of things or pictures in your mind? Even memories or flashes of memories?

Matt: Pictures or memories—he says, "yes," but does not specify the method.

PM: He just does. Okay, can Bosco hear me and respond to my questions?

Matt: Yes, he says that he can hear you because I can hear you.

PM: Got it. And can he respond (directly) to what I'm saying?

Matt: ... Yeah, like, I can hear what you're saying, it goes into my mind, and I can immediately just pass that on.

PM: Can Bosco help diagnose animals?

Matt: No, his knowledge is limited to what's in my brain.

PM: Does his knowledge span beyond this lifetime, or does he have knowledge about your past memories as well?

Matt: He says he knows what I know. But that he can put things together in ways I may not have considered.

PM: Okay, thank you, Bosco!

Matt: ... He says "you're welcome."

This exchange underscores the exploration of effective communication with the visible subconscious, with Bosco providing valuable insights. He stresses the importance of directness and specificity in requests, echoing principles outlined in sources such as Energy Gardener (2021).[1]

Bosco's versatility and willingness to assist align with the sentiments expressed by other visubs like Liam's and Laura's. As of now, there is no evidence to suggest that Bosco possesses the ability to engage with the visible subconscious minds of other individuals—at least not on this level. The intriguing possibility of facilitating such interactions remains uncharted territory, akin to unraveling the intricate mechanisms of a Chinese puzzle box.

Final Thoughts and Conclusion

In this chapter, we ventured into the realm of visible subconscious forms, uncovering invaluable insights into their potential to enrich our lives. It demonstrated the strong dependence and connection to the individual who possesses it, seemingly directly linked to the person's senses. Additionally, we learned the core principle of formulating requests to make them more agreeable to the subconscious.

Key Insights

- **The Power of Words:** We discovered that the choice of words when communicating with the visible subconscious profoundly influences the responses received. Direct and specific requests are crucial for effective communication.
- **The Extent of Capabilities:** Our interview with Bosco revealed a wide array of tasks that visible subconscious

forms can undertake. From channeling focus to easing motion sickness, their capabilities are remarkable and diverse.

- **Limitations of Communication:** It's essential to recognize that communication with visible subconscious forms, like Bosco, is limited to the individual they are connected with, in this case, Matt. Bosco's knowledge is confined to Matt's own, both conscious and unconscious, although his presence aids in organizing and clarifying this information.

- **Uncharted Territory:** While Bosco's abilities are impressive, the prospect of facilitating interactions between visible subconscious minds of different individuals remains unexplored. This tantalizing possibility presents a realm ripe for further investigation.

As we journey forward, the next chapter will explore Ethan's utilization of his visible subconscious, Blue, and further observations of its ongoing evolution. The exploration of the visible subconscious promises endless possibilities for personal growth and discovery.

9

THE COLOR OF CHANGE

 "Learn to consciously let go of the small stones you have accumulated all these years which have weighed you down collectively; travel light, travel strong, and focus on what matters."

— *PONZ MANANTAN*

After a two-week hiatus since our last meeting, Ethan and I reconvened for a casual check-in. He had a few questions on his mind, so we decided to catch up over a light meal at a nearby pub. As I drove, the radio DJ's announcement of National Ice Cream Sandwich Day briefly distracted me, but my craving for Fish and Chips remained steadfast that Tuesday.

Below is a transcription of a portion of our conversation during our meetup:

> **Ethan:** There isn't much to report lately due to recent events, but I do have a couple of questions. I'm a bit

confused about how often I should be connecting with
Blue. Should it be a regular occurrence, or should I wait
for specific situations to prompt her appearance? Those
are the questions I have.

PM: Alright.

Ethan: Should I always be the one initiating the
connection?

PM: Yes, because she's your subconscious. But have
there been times when she just showed up?

Ethan: No, and that's where I felt unsure, perhaps
because I haven't interacted with Blue lately. I wasn't
sure if she was supposed to appear spontaneously.

PM: No, because the way we've programmed the
subconscious is for you to initiate it.

Ethan: So if I initiate, she appears right away, yeah? She
pops up, and I get a clear image?

PM: Yes, because you and she are essentially one entity.
The subconscious typically remains in the background.
It might disrupt if it popped up randomly.

Ethan: I can see that. I just wasn't sure whether there
would be moments like that. There was one instance
that relates to this. I was in the backyard, reflecting on
the past week internally. I almost felt like I was having a
conversation with Blue, even though I didn't see her.
One thing I asked her was for her to find a way to
communicate with me verbally. It felt different, like she
was guiding me in a subtle way, like "Hey remember
this..." So, I'm not sure if that's related.

PM: Your subconscious is intimately connected to you,
perceiving your thoughts and emotions. Therefore,
during moments of self-reflection, any shifts you feel are
indications of your thoughts being registered by your
subconscious.

Ethan: Ah, that's starting to make sense now. It's like my conscious mind expresses a thought, and then the subconscious responds with the next one.

PM: Exactly. Normally, we have that inner voice—the subconscious—and by visually bringing it to the forefront, we've made it more noticeable and responsive. This heightened visibility might be why you sense something different. Sometimes, during certain activities, the subconscious might manifest visibly, as reported by some individuals who have experienced it. For instance, during intense contemplation, their visible subconscious might suddenly appear, prompting them to wonder about its presence. Often, they forget that during hypnosis, I mentioned the possibility of the subconscious showing up in situations where assistance might be needed. They overlook this aspect, leading to confusion when it manifests unexpectedly.

One participant experienced this, but his visible subconscious ceased appearing at random. Maybe it didn't want to annoy him. I recall interviewing a client's visible subconscious recently, inquiring about its capabilities and how to engage with it effectively to aid the individual. The response was straightforward: address the subconscious directly and articulate your needs specifically. This approach parallels hypnosis, where direct communication with the subconscious is necessary because it doesn't presume your desires. In this scenario, however, it operates with a heightened level of consciousness, being more prominent and responsive.

Ethan: So, essentially, you're guiding it towards the experience you want to have with your subconscious.

PM: Precisely. Being direct and specific in your requests ensures that your subconscious understands what you want, as it won't make assumptions about your intentions. That's how it can provide its best assistance.

Ethan: Got it.

PM: What other experiences have you had with Blue? What did you call her on?

Ethan: Well, there was a moment while I was driving on the freeway—I can't remember exactly where I was headed—but I called upon my subconscious for help with focus. However, I realized I needed to refine my goals and be more specific in my requests.

PM: Direct and specific, as the visible subconscious suggested.

Ethan: It felt weird, as if my message wasn't fully grasped, yet you understood precisely why. That was the moment in the car. It was brief. Initially, I asked, "Hey, can you assist with focus first, then motivation?" However, I quickly realized and amended my request. "Actually, help me maintain focus on that mental picture frame, that goal frame on the wall. Keep me anchored there." The picture—there's essentially nothing on that canvas. The essence I gleaned from her response was, "So, you're saying you're fixating on that empty canvas? You've set up the frame, but what exactly fills that picture?" I was like, "Fuck, you're right!" That blank canvas was merely a metaphor.

The vibe that I got from that discussion was that you just read about it, too, and you know how to teach people about it, too. The S.M.A.R.T. goal, you know. That stupid acronym for Specific, Measurable...

PM: ... Attainable, etc. Yeah.

Ethan: I was like, "No, you're right, goddamn it!" Yeah, so that was the moment in the car. And then there was another moment where I just briefly discussed, you know, what's around me and some questions. I was like, "Hey, Blue!" And she just appeared there, and I found myself pondering more about my future—things like my living situation, where I want to live, how much I want to earn. It was more like talking to myself aloud. Like, how do I envision my ideal lifestyle? So, I'm trying to go deeper into these questions, doing some mental math, and then circling back to my thoughts. I think that was the night before.

PM: And what insights did you gain?

Ethan: It's like, "Hey, I just want company." That was the main takeaway for me. It wasn't so much a conversation as it was me reaching out and having her sit with me, listening as I discussed my goals and aspirations.

PM: And how did she express herself?

Ethan: It's like, imagine having one of the worst nights of your life. You grab your phone and call someone, saying, "This just happened. I need you right now." They come over, and you spill everything without them saying much. It was like that with her—she had this intense listening expression, not just hearing the words but really absorbing them.

PM: Ah, because that's what you needed from her at the time. It was fulfilling its role.

Ethan: Exactly. I didn't have specific questions because I knew what I needed to work on. I just needed to express myself and have someone listen.

PM: And how did that experience affect you emotionally?

Ethan: You know, it wasn't too bad. And it got me thinking about different things. Like, if I were to start a side business, what would it be? I found myself revisiting those ideas I used to have but let slip away sometimes. It's like, "Okay, those thoughts used to occupy my mind a lot."

For my hobbies, whenever I encounter a problem or something that sparks an idea, I think, "How can I turn this into a business?" Then I jot down notes, make bullet points, and think about how I could make it work. But then I'd just add it to the stack of papers that have been sitting there forever. But recently, I had this realization, like, "Oh, I can actually do this!" It was refreshing to have those thoughts back.

PM: Alright.

Ethan: I think that was a positive aspect of it. Another part was about being more specific, like reminding myself, "Okay, if you want this type of job, what does your future vision of yourself look like? How many hours do you want to work? What does your work-life balance entail?" So, I've been pondering those questions.

And the more you focus and take action now, the faster you'll reach your goals. So, I think my goals extend beyond anything related to the VA or schooling.

And with that mindset, I feel like, "Okay, I can start investing in businesses and build an empire!" (making gun gestures with his fingers) Pew, pew, pew! But, of course, that's just step one!

So, I've got some work to do, like finishing school, attending night classes, and getting back into reading— I haven't read in almost a week. And then there's the workout routine. It's like I'm gaining more confidence. I have to remind myself, "The more you read, the more confident you'll feel working out on your own and doing it correctly." Because sometimes, the fear of doing it wrong holds me back from working out.

I just don't want to mess up my routine or fuck myself up, you know? So, I want to make sure I'm doing everything right, like ensuring I'm taking the proper nutrients. It's kind of nice.

PM: That's great! Before, you asked Blue to help motivate you with your workouts. Do you think Blue played a role in this change?

Ethan: I believe so, to some extent. Because I became more focused and started reading every single day. Not long after that, I really got into the habit of daily reading and made significant progress in the book. I'm about 35% through it now. There's not much left, but I just need to push through a bit more.

But there are like a thousand other goals swirling around. I thought, "Okay, this month, I need to at least finish the bookwork." They call it a gymternship—it's like an internship, but at a gym, I think. But I'm not sure how long it lasts, maybe two weeks. I just need to figure out the hours and what's involved with it.

And then I can take the test and start working, which will also improve my mood and, dude, make everything better. And if I decide to work at the gym, I'm already there, you know? I think it's partially helpful. I just need to be better at being more specific and consistent.

PM: Yeah. And also, you can reason with your subconscious why you want that. For example, "Help me be more motivated every time I do this because I want to..." or something like that.

Ethan: ... help me work out more so I can be able to lift 250 or whatever.

PM: Right. Or you can phrase it in the present tense. "... so I can lift 200 lbs. and feel better about myself..." or something similar. Because I think it's there to support you, whatever your goals are. So, if you explain the reasons behind your goals—to improve yourself, to feel more focused and confident—it becomes more supportive in helping you.

Ethan: That makes sense. And I think also, because of the past week, it was hard to accept any help. I've been thinking a lot about that, too. It really threw me off balance. I was like, "No, I won't let it affect me. I will not get knocked off the rocker." But it definitely did.

PM: Just like when you requested to change the taste of the drink from orange to grape? It was like, "Okay, fine, I'll change it. Whatever!"

Ethan: That was interesting, definitely, especially the switch from orange to grape. It was quite a drastic change. It was weird!

PM: It could be useful for people working on weight loss. For those who want to avoid certain foods that trigger cravings—whether it's the crunchiness, texture, or saltiness—changing those elements to make them less pleasurable, less salty, etc., can help you achieve your goals. Through hypnosis, I've encountered these issues with my clients. So, by making those changes, it alters how the mind perceives the food.

Ethan: That's a great point! I should try that with tomatoes!

PM: It's all about changing the perception of food. Any other questions from our previous discussions?

Ethan: No, we knocked those out pretty quick.

PM: Any other goals you're aiming for now that you've learned some tips?

Ethan: I've been working on that too. Since my mental health has improved, I want to explore new things, try different activities. I've started seeing a therapist, and I've found it beneficial. There are some groups through the VA where you can try various activities. For example, they offer yoga classes—I might give that a shot and see how much my core needs work. I've been slacking on my workouts, but I need to get back into it. So, that's something I'm going to try.

And as for my new endeavor, I want to challenge myself

to try something new every week, or maybe just a variation of something different. Incorporating that variety into my routine once a week.

PM: That sounds like a great plan!

I shared with Ethan Matt's tale, recounting how Matt sought Bosco's counsel to stay committed to his daily supplement regimen, providing a source of motivation through the visub. Many people embrace supplements to support their weight loss goals, but the monotony of prolonged intake can lead to apathy. The visub emerged as a beacon of motivation in this scenario.

Additionally, I recounted the account of the inflamed vein incident, illustrating how the visub diligently worked to assist in its healing process.

Ethan: You know, I really need to keep that in mind, especially during massages. Mistakes tend to reveal themselves pretty quickly. If you're off on your technique, your hands or wrists will start to feel it. I noticed some discomfort in my wrists, and I thought, "I need to correct this immediately. Use the proper technique, so I don't end up with chronic pain down the line." So, I think the healing aspect would definitely be beneficial.

PM: Absolutely, quicker healing and pain relief.

Ethan: Pain relief was a bit trickier to gauge. I only noticed a slight improvement in one or two spots, while everywhere else, the discomfort persisted. That part was a bit more challenging for me.

PM: I see. Well, if you're up for it, we can give it a try now. I'll gently pinch you.

Ethan: Sure, let's see how it goes. (He stretches his arm out on the table, revealing a tattoo on his forearm.)

PM: So, what was her response?

Ethan: She said, "Okay."

PM: What exactly did you ask her?

Ethan: I asked her, "Blue, make it so I feel no pain on my forearm with the tattoo."

PM: Alright, let's see if that works. I'll pinch you on the tattooed area now...

Ethan: I can barely feel it. It's like... with taste, it worked, but not with sensation. Does that make sense?

PM: Pain might not disappear entirely, but it could decrease significantly, maybe from a 10 to a 1.

Ethan: Ah, got it! That makes sense now! It's a big difference when... yeah, exactly!

PM: Now, can you feel it outside the tattoo? (pinching just outside the tattoo)

Ethan: Oh, definitely!

PM: And inside the tattoo? (pinching inside the tattoo again)

Ethan: It's like a 10 to 1 difference! Yeah!

PM: See?

Ethan: Yeah, okay, now I see what you're talking about!Ah....

PM: Those were hard pinches!

Ethan: Yeah, I see what you mean now! I thought it was supposed to completely vanish when I felt it. The first time, I was like, "Hmm, I still feel it." So, I kind of fixated on that, thinking, "If I feel anything, it's not working." But now it makes a lot more sense!

PM: There's a distinction between reducing pain and numbing the area. Numbing means you won't feel pain, but you'll feel the sensation on the skin. I tested that too, numbing the area and then poking or pinching it.

Ethan: Ah, interesting!

PM: It's like using anesthetics.

Ethan: Got it, makes sense.

PM: Pain management and numbing—analgesia. Some people are allergic to anesthetics, so they turn to hypnosis for a similar effect before surgery.

Ethan: That's wild!

PM: Yeah, they get hypnotized instead of receiving anesthesia.

Ethan: It's like going into surgery without medication.

PM: Exactly. But with you and Blue, it's like, "Okay, go for it!" Pretty quick, right?

Ethan: Definitely! It almost makes you want to test it more, but you also don't want to hurt yourself, you know? "Let's give this a try cautiously!"

PM: Yup, gotta tread carefully! Oh, about headaches! I'm not sure if I mentioned it before—one person got the COVID-19 booster shot.

Ethan: Yeah, you did mention it! It acted like a shortcut, right? Helped with his sinuses, I recall?

PM: It helped alleviate the side effects. He felt a warm sensation on his forehead, and his headache decreased by around 90%. That quick! Even the injection area on his left arm, which was painful, warmed up, and the pain vanished. However, his fever remained unaffected. But those were significant improvements.

Ethan: Makes sense. Whatever works in that situation, right?

PM: Definitely! He experienced another headache at a different time, so he called upon his subconscious for help again. Same result—it vanished. He said he relied on it a few times without any medication, which is fantastic! So, you might want to give it a shot. Experiment more!

Ethan: Yeah, I will. I think this week will be different.

PM: Uh-huh. Use Blue. Remember, I gave you a Ferrari. Don't use it just to run errands! Make the most of it!

Ethan: (laughing) You are correct! I love that analogy! That's pretty funny! It's a good one!

Hey, I noticed Blue has been sitting most of the time lately.

PM: How is she sitting?

Ethan: Cross-legged, just looking at me like, "What are you going to say? What do you need help with?"

PM: That's interesting! Has this been happening for a few days?

Ethan: Sometimes, when I need to talk, she's in that position or something similar. It's happened about four times now. I wonder if her leg is bothering her.

PM: Maybe. Have you noticed anything else different?

Ethan: No, not really.

PM: (remembering Ethan's mention of nice toenails from a previous conversation) You've never seen her toenails before, have you?

Ethan: No, but as we talked about it, I got this image of vibrant green toenails. I didn't even have to ask her. I was like, "Oh, crap, I think I already know!" And she responds, "There, those are my feet I showed you!" So, I saw translucent nails, watery crystal blue. It would be fascinating to see and hear her speak. But at the same time, like I mentioned the other day, I didn't feel like myself. I did ask recently, "Can you communicate with words?" So, I'm curious.

PM: How do you think verbal communication with her would impact you?

Ethan: I think it would be a powerful way to internally process things. When you can hear it and talk it out, it's like having a conversation with yourself but from a different perspective. Two minds are better than one, to a certain extent. It's like fostering communication between different parts of your brain. I like that idea, improving communication with myself.

PM: I was wondering if there's something the subconscious knows that might affect you, which is why she's not using words.

Ethan: Hmmm…

PM: Because sometimes, there might be something that we're unaware of how it might affect us. One participant hears words from her visible subconscious and sees less gestures—verbal communication seems to be her preferred method, which might work better for her. I don't know.

Ethan: I can see that. Often, I prefer actions over words when it comes to communication. That's significant for me, like the five love languages. Mine is quality time, which outweighs everything else, except gift-giving, which is at 1%. I'd rather spend time with someone than receive gifts or hear words. I know, it's odd.

PM: I can somehow see why your subconscious communicates that way. It might be better for you that way.

Ethan: Well, I like the look. Definitely thought-provoking, isn't it?

PM: Yeah, indeed.

Just then, Ethan's phone rang. As he glanced at the screen, his expression shifted, and it seemed as if all the joy drained out from him. With a heavy sigh, he showed me the caller's name before answering the call—it was his ex-wife. After their brief conversation, he reluctantly informed me that he had to leave.

Ethan and his wife had drifted apart mainly due to her uncontrollable substance abuse. Despite his earnest attempts to mend their relationship, her addiction persisted, forcing Ethan to establish emotional boundaries to safeguard himself.

Nevertheless, his ex-wife frequently turned to him for assistance in various matters, and out of a sense of obligation, Ethan consistently lent a helping hand. Yet, he keenly sensed her lack of gratitude for his endeavors, and encountering her often left him grappling with unnecessary emotional distress. Ethan had begun to acknowledge the toll this persistent situation had exacted on his mental health.

A few days later, Ethan reached out to set up another face-to-face meeting, indicating he had additional updates to discuss. He shared a drawing he had created of Blue.

BLUE

Drawing of Blue with long flowing hair and a belly button

Ethan: Blue's height has changed; she's now around 5'4." Also, I felt like there was an actual conversation that happened. It was like it was my voice, but different somehow.

PM: Different in what way?

Ethan: It's hard to explain. It was like my voice, but with a twist. I almost felt like I was talking to myself, but not quite. It was a strange moment today. I found myself saying, "Blue, make it so..." and then she responded, "Okay, I'll do that." It was like I was talking to myself, but not really.

PM: So, it was your voice, but slightly altered?

Ethan: Yeah, exactly. It felt like me, but not entirely. It was odd.

PM: Well, what do you think about that?

Ethan: I don't know yet.

PM: You wanted Blue to have a voice, right?

Ethan: Yeah, I did. I wanted her to be able to talk, but now that it's happening, it's kind of weird. It feels like I'm just talking to myself.

PM: In your voice, but with a twist.

Ethan: Right. It's like my subconscious is speaking, but with a different tone.

PM: That's actually quite common with visible subconscious manifestations. Some people hear their subconscious with a deeper voice, while others experience a slightly altered version of their own voice.

Ethan: Yeah. The best way I could think of it is like, if I had to dress up like a woman and try to talk like one, that's how it came out. And it threw me off. I'm like, "Okay."

PM: Have you thought about asking Blue to change her voice to something else?

Ethan: I've considered it. Maybe I could sift through different female voices until I find one that I like, and then ask Blue to use that. That way, I'll know it's her when she speaks. But the whole thing is just... weird.

PM: At least you recognize it as your subconscious

speaking, rather than an unfamiliar voice. You can always ask her to change it later if you decide.

Ethan: Yeah, for now, I think I'll stick with it. Let me mull it over a bit more.

PM: Sounds like a plan.

Ethan: Yeah. I've been experimenting this week and taking notes. I just forgot to update you until now. But since we're on the topic of Blue, I figured we should talk again. I added two more things, and it took me a while to figure out how to ask properly.

PM: That's good progress.

Ethan: Right. Becoming more specific and like," This is also why I want this." Yeah.

PM: I'm proud of you, Ethan!

Ethan: Thanks! I was hoping you would be!

PM: It's like having a different class. Learning about something new. Mastering it.

Ethan: Yeah. It's like an inner you, but with a twist, you know? It's just another way to understand yourself better.

PM: Have you reduced the number of cigarettes that you smoke?

Ethan: Honestly, it has decreased a bit, but...

PM: By how much?

Ethan: Maybe one to three cigarettes. Not a significant change where I'm proud of myself, but there's been a small improvement.

PM: So, you're not ready to quit yet?

Ethan: I still use it, especially when dealing with my ex. It's become a coping mechanism for me. I started smoking during my deployment when I was around 20 or 21. It helped a lot back then, and now it's just something I find comforting, like "Ah!"

PM: Is there anything else you can find that provides a

similar sense of comfort that would be the equivalent of "Ah?"

Ethan: Yes, I have. There was a time when I quit for about ten and a half months. Engaging in physical activities helped me feel better. But the stress from my marriage made me say, "Fuck it! I'm going to smoke again because it's so hard to deal with this shit!" I relapsed. Now that I'm out of that situation, I want to focus on eliminating things that aren't beneficial for me.

PM: So, how do you plan to tackle the smoking?

Ethan: It's not my main priority right now. I've been focusing on other things, like my interactions with my ex. I've made it clear to myself and Blue that I need to stay disciplined and avoid contact with her. While having a conversation with Blue, I was specific when I said, "Hey, Blue. I want to make sure that I don't come in contact with her, I stay away from her, and I focus on myself because it is way better for me. Every time I give in, it has a negative impact on me, and this is why I need to stay away from her. I need to make sure that I don't go back to that." And that's when I got that "Okay, I got you." I need to break that pattern.

PM: That sounds like a healthy approach.

Ethan: Yeah, it's a work in progress. I've been experimenting with communicating with Blue more effectively. For instance, I asked her to alleviate the pain in my wrist. I was outside, and my wrist was hurting, so I said, "Hey, Blue. Will you mitigate this pain where it's not as bad anymore?" And, literally, it decreased! Within three to five seconds, there was this weird feeling on my wrist and the pain got minimized!" It was probably a five, and then it went to a one. I was like, "That feels great!"

PM: That's impressive! It shows that your subconscious mind is capable of making changes.

Ethan: Uh-huh. Right. And I'm going to backtrack. So, earlier in the week, after we met last time, I brought her to me because I wanted to talk about this. But each time I did that, I either talked or, like, nothing happened. I was just like, "Hey, Blue! I want you here because I want to talk about something." And I would start talking, but then I would stop. And nothing would come of it. It was okay; she was just in the presence.

PM: She was just listening, without interacting.

Ethan: Exactly. Earlier in the week, I tried to communicate with her, but nothing really happened. I wasn't in the right mindset. But recently, I've been more specific in my requests. Like, today, I talked to her about my workout routine and was specific about it. I said, "Blue, I want to work out at least five days a week, maybe six, but it has to be at least five days a week." I also stated the reasons, like when I said, "Hey, Blue. I want to work out because of X, Y, and Z. I want to work out this; I want to look this certain way; it's going to make me feel better; this is why…" And then I got an "Okay." It took some time to articulate my goals clearly, but eventually, I got her approval.

PM: It seems like you're making progress in communicating with your subconscious.

Ethan: Yeah, I'm starting to see the benefits. I've been sticking to my workout for the past few days, so that's a good sign. I want to keep that motivation and discipline up.

PM: How does your current workout routine differ from what you were doing before you consulted Blue?

Ethan: I'd say the major shift came after opening up to her about my ex and everything. I no longer feel this obligation to someone who drained so much from my life because I've realized I had other responsibilities, including to myself. It's been a journey of self-discovery. I used to feel responsible for her because she couldn't fend for herself. But now, I understand that responsibility can manifest in other areas of my life. That's been the most significant change I've noticed. Now that weight's lifted, it's easier to focus. I've been craving this clarity. Maybe it's because I've made the decision to cut my ex out of my life for now. So now, when I want to buckle down and study, I can do just that without worrying about her.

PM: So, you're feeling more focused now after confiding in Blue and without the compulsion to come to your ex's rescue. They call it the rescuer complex. And you feel more valued as a result?

Ethan: Exactly. I relish that feeling. I feel good about myself. Like, "Hey, I'm always the first person she turns to when things go awry." I've always been that guy. And I like that feeling. But I also recognize it's not healthy to derive that validation solely from her.

PM: That's understandable. What was the shift like for you after consulting Blue? How different was the feeling?

Ethan: Relief. It felt like a weight lifted off my shoulders.

PM: How do you respond now when your ex-wife reaches out to you?

Ethan: We've ceased communication. She's unblocked for tonight, but come tomorrow, she'll be blocked again. It's a necessary measure to ensure no contact right now.

PM: And you're at peace with that decision now?

Ethan: About 80-20. A part of me still cares deeply for her well-being, given our decade-long marriage. But I've learned to separate that. I'm okay with it now. It's like, "I helped you, and you still disrespected me beyond a reasonable doubt." I mean, that hits me so much. After that, and everything? No! Like, If I come back to you, I'm a piece of shit? No! There's no excuse for me to keep helping you anymore.

Now my focus is on self-improvement and charting the course for my own future. To focus on that picture frame of where I want to be. I'm still in the process of setting new goals.

Also, with school, I want to be the person who people can come to and ask a question. It's like, "Hey, I got you! This is what it is..." you know? That's where I see myself, and I want that. It is what I'm working on and where Blue has been helping with what I've been asking.

PM: And since consulting Blue, have you noticed a difference in your focus?

Ethan: It's only been a couple of days, so it's still early days. But I've been hitting the books yesterday and today, and I'm also planning to tackle my other school-work. And so, it's motivating me to think of different ways of getting better at it. Like, "OK, I need to be better about, finance, maybe get them both to where I can have time to study, workout, all that kind of stuff."

PM: Is it becoming easier for you now?

Ethan: Definitely!

PM: Thank you, Blue!

Ethan: Absolutely! She's been a game-changer. And she's hot! So, I appreciate it! It's a win-win. Feeling better, being better, and having Blue around as a very nice human being that I like to look at—it's not a bad deal at all. This past week has been quite the journey. Looking forward to what's next and I'll keep you updated with more timely texts this time.

PM: Your progress is truly appreciated.

Ethan: I've realized this week that all I have to do is ask. It's as simple as that.

PM: Absolutely!

Ethan: And since our last meeting, I've been more proactive. I'm learning to be more specific with my requests, which seems to yield more tailored results. So, I'm working on that. I took some time earlier today to talk through the specifics. Like, "Okay, this is this... do this... with this... on top of this... because of this... and this is why you also want to do it. Do you understand? Okay! Alright, cool! I'm glad we're both on the same page!" Now I get it!

PM: Cool!

Final Thoughts and Conclusion

This chapter provides a captivating insight into Ethan's journey alongside his visible subconscious, Blue. Their dynamic relationship highlights the potential for introspection and clear communication to facilitate growth and development. Ethan's experiences serve as a testament to the profound influence of the subconscious mind on one's life trajectory.

Key Insights and Developments

- **Ethan's Desire for Blue to Speak:** Ethan expresses his desire for Blue to communicate with him using words, as it would provide a different way for him to work through his thoughts and feelings.
- **Blue's Emerging Voice:** Blue eventually begins to speak, but her voice sounds similar to Ethan's, albeit slightly different. Though Ethan asked for this to

happen, it surprises and intrigues him, and he contemplates the possibility of customizing Blue's voice to something unique.

- **Progress in Smoking Reduction:** Ethan discusses his progress in curbing his smoking habit. With Blue's help, he has managed to smoke fewer cigarettes each day. While specific reduction targets remain undefined, Ethan acknowledges the positive impact of this progress.

- **Enhanced Focus and Aspirations:** Ethan's interactions with Blue help him focus on his goals and aspirations. He experiences increased clarity and motivation in various aspects of his life, including academic pursuits and physical fitness endeavors.

- **Pain Relief:** Ethan also turns to Blue for help with physical discomfort, such as wrist pain from massage work. Blue's help provides relief and contributes to Ethan's overall well-being.

- **The Power of Precision in Communication:** Ethan learns that the more specific and direct he can be in his requests to Blue, the more effective Blue's responses become. Being precise in his communication with his subconscious helps him achieve his goals more efficiently.

- **Self-Discipline and Personal Growth:** Ethan's commitment to self-discipline and personal growth shines through. With Blue's support, he focuses on healthier habits like regular exercise and improved study routines.

- **Distancing from Unhealthy Relationships:** With Blue's support, Ethan is better able to distance himself from unhealthy relationships, particularly with his ex-wife. This allows him to prioritize his own well-being and personal development.

- **Transformation Through Inner Dialogue:** The chapter underscores the transformative power of seeking help from within. Ethan's conversations with Blue act as a catalyst for positive changes in his life, and he begins to tap into the potential of his subconscious mind.

Ethan's story reminds us that with determination, self-awareness, and a willingness to explore the depths of our own consciousness, we can embark on a journey of self-discovery and transformation, ultimately leading to a more fulfilling and purpose-driven existence.

In the next chapter, we'll explore some compelling questions: Can the visible subconscious engage in profound conversations? Can it provide fitting responses? How does our subconscious evolve with our experiences? And what are the consequences if we disregard its guidance? Dive in to uncover these intriguing topics!

10

SEEING THE VOICE OF REASON

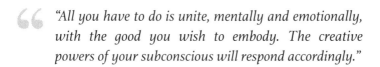 *"All you have to do is unite, mentally and emotionally, with the good you wish to embody. The creative powers of your subconscious will respond accordingly."*

— *JOSEPH MURPHY*

In this brief check-in with Laura, she underscored the significance of Joseph, her visible subconscious, and his impact on her life. Throughout our conversation, she reflected on moments where she hadn't fully embraced Joseph's guidance and candidly discussed her personal struggles.

She highlights the benefits of tapping into her visible subconscious and shares creative ways she has applied it in practical situations.

Here's the transcript of most of what we talked about.

PM: How's everything? What's different?
Laura: Well, Ponz, I wish I had better news for you. But I was just a crazy lady! It's like there's always something.

PM: A crazy lady?

Laura: Yeah, when I left your office, I felt really happy. But then, I don't know, it's like I don't tap into my subconscious. I let myself spiral until I can't handle it anymore! Then I decide, "Okay, time to be happy now." I just start overthinking everything, finding reasons for things to go wrong instead of right. Does that make sense? And then, after driving myself and my partner crazy with negativity, I finally thought, "Okay, Joseph, I just want to be happy now." That's when I decided to call on my subconscious mind! (laughs)

PM: So, when you called on Joseph, your visible subconscious, what did you discuss or ask about?

Laura: Oh, I talked about the whole situation with selling the house and our contract for the new place. I asked, "Is everything going to be okay?" And the answer was, "Yes, everything will be okay because no matter what, we're still moving to the new place!" So, I realized I have no reason not to be happy.

PM: Uh-huh. But...

Laura: But it took me all week, Ponz, to reach that conclusion! I had to stop dwelling on the what-ifs and focus on the fact that there really are no what-ifs! I have no reason to be fixated on uncertainties, even if there's still work to be done in the house.

PM: But then you made the decision to be happy now.

Laura: Yeah, I mean, I guess it didn't take as long as it could have. A week isn't too bad, right? I mean, it could have dragged on for a month, but...

PM: ... but usually, it would take you longer than that?

Laura: Yeah, now I'm just like, "No matter what, we're moving to the new place." So... I don't have any reason not to be happy, you know?

PM: That's right.

Laura: So, I'm just thinking, "Why did I waste all those days focusing on 'what if this happens,' 'what if we need to do that'..." and...

PM: ... and?

Laura: I didn't need to be like that.

PM: That's right. And how long were you worried about those things? Even before our session?

Laura: Oh, yeah!

PM: And now it is a shorter timeframe. Have you been having better insights? More clarity?

Laura: I think so. Well, let's see how this week goes. But today has been amazing! My partner thinks I'm completely nuts, says I'm batshit crazy! (laughs uncontrollably) I told him maybe he should give you the update. But he loves me, he said. No matter what. He even told me, "Call Joseph!" (continues to laugh)

PM: Yeah, why not? So, you haven't been utilizing Joseph much.

Laura: No, Ponz, why haven't I? What's holding me back? I put myself through the wringer before I even think, "Okay, time to be happy."

PM: Hmmm.... are you a perfectionist?

Laura: I think I am. My first husband used to say that about me.

We briefly digressed to discuss her worries before returning to our main conversation.

PM: How about in those moments when you encounter those challenges, do you also call on your subconscious mind? You often know what's wrong and how it should be. Maybe you could instruct your subconscious to help you make things right. Be more adaptable and accepting of change, understanding that sometimes near enough is good enough, and things don't have to be perfect every time. Something like that.

Laura: Alright.

PM: Since your subconscious is connected to your thoughts, even those deeply ingrained or habitual, it could assist in altering them. Rather than repeatedly affirming how things should be, why not seek your (visible) subconscious's help in making those changes? It could speed up the process of reshaping those thoughts.

Laura: I understand.

PM: Have there been other occasions when you've called on Joseph and requested his assistance?

Laura: No, I've been pretty awful this week, Ponz. My partner can vouch for that. I even mentioned he suggested I call Joseph! (brief laughter) Let me elaborate on Joseph's significance. I named my subconscious Joseph because my best friend once dated someone named Joseph, and he always brought her immense happiness. The way she radiated joy is how I always want to feel—just like that. Like Joseph! That's what happiness means to me.

PM: And did you experience that happiness when you were in the office?

Laura: Yeah! It's like the happiness I saw on her face and heard in her voice. I want to feel that way all the time!

PM: Uh-huh. Then maybe you should call on Joseph more often! (both laughing) It seems like a solution! Stop worrying about things!

Laura: Yeah, you're absolutely right!

PM: How does Joseph's voice sound? Does he communicate with words, gestures, or sounds?

Laura: I feel like Joseph actually speaks to me, Ponz. Is that strange? Am I crazy for thinking so?

PM: No. I'm just curious. What does the voice sound like?

Laura: The accent is kind of like Dominican... almost. A Dominican accent.

PM: So, it sounds like a real person.

Laura: Yeah!

PM: Okay. Well, you're not crazy because others with visible subconscious also hear a voice. Sometimes it's in their own voice, only deeper or altered in some way. But it can also communicate through sounds, pictures, or gestures—like nodding for yes or no. It varies. But hearing a voice from the subconscious when it communicates with you is perfectly normal.

Laura: Okay. So, I'm not completely batshit crazy! (bursts out laughing)

PM: No, maybe it's using more words because that's easier for you both to understand each other. It's a way of communication with your subconscious. It depends, but you're not crazy!

Laura: Alright. Okay. Oh my god!

PM: I recall you mentioning before that you had a goal related to... was it weight loss or waking up early?

Laura: Yeah, it's about waking up! And yes, he's been helping me with that. But ummm... guess what?

PM: What?

Laura: I haven't been consistent with it (referring to working out). We've been so busy working on the house! (laughs, feeling embarrassed)

PM: Oh, that's understandable. But he has been waking you up, you mentioned?

Laura: Yes! He wakes me up!

PM: How does he do that?

Laura: I don't know, it's like I just automatically... it's as if he says, "It's time for you to wake up!"

PM: Really? That's fantastic!

Laura: And it's even before my alarm goes off!

PM: That's what I thought when you mentioned it earlier. It's amazing how he influences or guides your body.

Laura: Yeah!

PM: Have there been any other ways he's been assisting or communicating with you besides waking you up?

Laura: I think there have been moments where, instead of getting into arguments, it's almost like I hear a voice saying, "Just stay quiet, don't say anything."

PM: Ah, that must be Joseph. Your subconscious is advising you. See? You're tuning into your inner voice!

Laura: I believe it is Joseph, guiding me to keep quiet.

PM: Yes, your inner voice. But how would you typically respond without Joseph's guidance?

Laura: Oh, I'd open my mouth, like I always do! (laughs heartily)

PM: But now you're more restrained because of that inner voice reminding you.

Laura: Yeah!

PM: That's progress!

Laura: Yeah... you got me started somewhere, I guess!

PM: Yeah, that's true! Have you noticed any other ways he's been helping you, or anything different?

Laura: I haven't really noticed anything different.

PM: Understandable, since you haven't been using him much this week.

Laura: No, I haven't, not this week. Let's see what next week brings. Maybe I'll actually get out of bed and hop on to my workout machine.

Laura's fixation on relocating from her residence understandably hindered progress on some of her objectives, yet she asserts a clear perception of Joseph, hearing him speak with a distinct Dominican accent. While skeptics may dismiss this as mere hallucination, others question how an entity invisible to outsiders could influence her thoughts and actions. Some propose it could be a placebo effect, where the belief in its efficacy drives positive changes irrespective of its tangible reality, like being given a sugar pill, believing it's the actual treatment, and then the body producing the same chemicals as the supposed medication. Dr. Dispenza (2014) argued in his book *You Are The Placebo: Making Your Mind Matter* that we ourselves can serve as the placebo, shaping our experiences through the power of our minds.[1]

> **PM:** Let me ask you something. When you're in your normal state of mind and you call Joseph, do you notice any difference in your thought process? Does it feel like you're using more of your processor or mental resources?
>
> **Laura:** When I think of Joseph, even if I'm not actively calling on him, it calms me down and makes me want to relax more. It helps me stay unfrazzled.
>
> **PM:** That's good to hear! What about when you're speaking to Joseph, like with your eyes closed? Does that process feel different? Someone mentioned that when they call on their subconscious and see it, it feels like their mind is tackling a tough puzzle, or they're using more (brain) power. Does it feel like that for you, too? It might be different for each person.
>
> **Laura:** I haven't really thought about it. I don't feel like I'm using more mental power.
>
> **PM:** Fair enough. I think I understand now. The person who mentioned it was seeing it with their eyes open, so that might require more mental effort compared to having your eyes closed.

Laura: Yeah, that makes sense.

PM: Just one more question. When Joseph was singing "God Bless America," which voice was he using?

Laura: What do you mean by which voice?

PM: I mean, was he singing in his Dominican voice?

Laura: Oh, it was awful! He was trying to sing in my voice. It was terrible!

PM: Oh, so it was in your voice!

Laura: Yeah. But it sounded just as bad as when I sing!

PM: I haven't heard you sing, but now I'm curious!

Laura: Trust me, you don't want to. It's really bad!

PM: So, if you were to sing, would you sound like that?

Laura: Oh, yeah. It's really awful!

PM: Yeah? Maybe we should go to Karaoke sometime!

Laura: (bursting out laughing)

PM: I'm kidding. So, Laura, your homework is to do your best to utilize Joseph more.

Laura: Okay. That should be easy homework.

PM: Do you have questions?

Laura: No. I'm actually glad I did this!

PM: That's good! I gave you a Ferrari, Laura, use it! Don't just use it to go to the grocery store!

Laura: (laughing) Okay! Got it!

PM: Just play around. Take advantage of it.

Laura: I will. I definitely will!

IT HAS BEEN A MONTH SINCE LAURA'S INITIAL SESSION, AND NOW it's time for another brief check-in.

PM: How's everything with you and Joseph? How have you been using Joseph?

Laura: Well, I've been relying on him most of the time.

But there are moments where I just don't call on him when I should. Recently, there was a moment at work where we had a minor crisis with our vendor. Part of what I was responsible for was impacted or was going to be impacted. I found myself stressed and anxious over nothing, much like with my husband.

My husband keeps reminding me about Joseph, saying, "Laura, you have to call Joseph!" But I resist reaching out to him.

PM: Ah, he knows what to say; he knows what to do.

Laura: Yeah, he does, but I don't know why I put myself through it. It was unnecessary stress in the end. Back in New York, our company's philosophy was, "Unless somebody's going to die, it can wait, and it's not that important." Right? Like, unless, you know, somebody's going to die, don't let it impact you so negatively. And I think I threw out everything in the window that day. The next day, I realized my mistake and called on Joseph, admitting, "I was wrong to do that." Even though I knew it was wrong, I still did it.

PM: So, you were aware it was wrong, but you went ahead and did it anyway.

Laura: Yeah, I guess Joseph was right. It's like I knew better, but I still went ahead. I have this perfectionist streak where everything has to be just right, and I can't rest until it is. I feel this need to ensure everything is okay, even though I already know it is. That day, it felt like everyone was dumping their responsibilities on me, and I didn't know how to push back or express my frustration. It's not really in my nature to confront people like that, so I just took it all on myself. It was incredibly stressful.

PM: So, you ended up assuming all the responsibility.

Laura: Yeah, and I shouldn't have. Maybe that was the battle.

PM: But initially, you discussed it with Joseph. What did he say?

Laura: Well, Joseph is always the voice of reason, but I just wasn't listening! He kept telling me, "Laura, you shouldn't be doing this. Laura, you can't handle all of this. Laura, don't stress over it," but I ignored his advice.

PM: So, will you listen to Joseph more next time, now that you realize that?

Laura: Of course! (chuckles) Yes, I'll listen to Joseph because he always seems to be right! (Laughs) It's not really my style, and... I don't know! My dad used to say I was stubborn and never listened. I guess now, looking back, I see what he meant. Like, I don't even listen to myself! So yeah, I think I get what my dad was trying to say.

PM: Uh-huh. That's a positive development because you're recognizing it better now, based on your experiences.

Laura: That's true. Yeah!

PM: Yeah. Maybe you can ask Joseph to help you listen to him more? Or to help you refrain from doing something you know you shouldn't?

Laura: Right.

PM: Let's see if your subconscious can make adjustments to make it easier for you to resist doing what you know isn't right.

Laura: Yeah, and to delegate tasks back to those who should be handling them. That's a good idea!

PM: Not taking on what isn't your responsibility. Understanding the boundaries between your responsibilities and others'. Not overstepping those boundaries or assuming too much responsibility. See how Joseph responds if you ask him to assist you with that.

Laura: Okay... I'm jotting down notes...

PM: Because we know he can influence thoughts and perspectives, altering the way we perceive things. So, if you ask him, your subconscious, he might make some changes. You'll likely notice it. And you'll say, "Yes!!! I resisted because I knew it wasn't right! And you were so right, Joseph!"

Laura: (laughs) Yeah, Joseph always seems right to me.

PM: It's good to hear that you've been utilizing Joseph! Have there been other instances when you've relied on him?

Laura: Well, I still turn to Joseph for motivation to work out. I haven't been consistent every day, but every other day, I'm committed. I feel motivated. Apart from the work setback, I think I've been doing pretty well with Joseph! He's been keeping me on track!

PM: That's fantastic!

Laura: I still feel joyful. Maybe it's because I'm moving out of here; I'm excited about that! Moving to a different state feels like a fresh start. Overall, I've been happier lately. I think it's partly because of the sunshine and longer days. It just feels like a more joyful time, with less darkness overall.

In general, I just think I'm a different person! And then there's Joseph. I think it's a combination of everything changing. Everything's going to be completely different!

PM: That's wonderful! If you hadn't known Joseph before, how do you think the past month would have been?

Laura: Oh, the past month would have been tough. Instead of focusing on the positives, I'd probably dwell on the negatives, as my partner often points out. But I haven't been doing that lately, I don't think.

PM: And you believe Joseph has played a significant role in that?

Laura: Yeah! When I let him. Sometimes I don't listen to myself, like last week.

PM: We're always learning from ourselves, constantly improving.

Laura: That's true, yeah. I feel like I'm getting better. I can see the improvement!

PM: That's great! Are there any other areas where you think Joseph could help you?

Laura: Still with my workout routine, and managing interactions with my partner, like agreeing to disagree. I've definitely gotten better at that. But one thing I still struggle with is asserting myself when something isn't my responsibility, especially with friends. Like, when they let me down, I need to express how I feel. Recently, a friend stood me up, and I didn't confront her about it. I just assumed she had her reasons, but I think I need to address it. That's something I haven't improved on, and I think Joseph could help me with that.

PM: Maybe it's a good start to avoid jumping to conclusions and giving them the benefit of the doubt. You can ask her what happened and express your feelings about it. How do you think you could ask Joseph to assist you with that?

Laura: I guess, to have more confidence that I can talk to her. If someone is truly your friend, you should feel comfortable expressing yourself, right?

PM: Absolutely.

Laura: And they should be open to hearing how I felt. But I guess I lack confidence in expressing myself.

Driving all the way to the city and then being stood up
—it's a complete disregard for my time.

PM: Right. Unless there's a valid reason. But you don't
know yet why she didn't show up.

Laura: Right. So... yeah! (contemplating) I'm going to
talk to her. Because I think I need to address it.

PM: Uh-huh! And would you like a boost of self-
confidence?

Laura: I'll be like, "Joseph, please help?"

PM: Yeah, you can ask Joseph to help you with that and
let me know how it goes.

Laura: I'll keep you posted.

PM: Perfect! And I recall you mentioning before that
Joseph can change how his appearance depending on
what you need. Has he been changing his form, or is it
still the same?

Laura: It's still the same. He's still appearing as
Dominican.

PM: And does he look human-like when you see him?

Laura: Yes, he appears human, with very dark
complexion.

PM: With a Dominican accent.

Laura: Yeah.

PM: Is it like having a real friend, in a way?

Laura: Almost like having an alter ego, I guess. It's actually pretty cool! I think it is!

PM: Yeah. I think only a few people have that level of
interactivity with their subconscious. Just keep utilizing
Joseph. And remember, if you have a problem, you
probably know how to solve it or what's wrong. You can
ask him for help in improving whatever aspect you're
struggling with. And remember, he can also influence
bodily functions.

Laura: If I look in the mirror and see wrinkles, can

Joseph just make them disappear so I don't have to see them anymore? Is that possible?

PM: Yeah... he'd probably joke, "Oh, I'm not a genie!"

Laura: (laughs heartily)

PM: Just kidding!

Laura: Oh, you got me!

PM: Well, you can try. Who knows, it might work!

Laura: I'll give it a shot, Ponz!

PM: Yes! Perfect! I'm glad that you're utilizing him more. You're motivated and choosing to be happier more often.

Laura: Yes, that's the best approach right now.

PM: Yeah, that's true!

Final Thoughts and Conclusion

In this continuation of Laura's journey with her visible subconscious, we've witnessed her ongoing exploration of the wisdom and guidance embodied by Joseph. As Laura navigates the challenges of daily life, she learns to rely on her visible subconscious more frequently, discovering its remarkable capacity to influence her thoughts, perspectives, and even bodily functions. While not a magical fix, the visible subconscious can serve as a valuable resource for personal growth and self-improvement. Through her experiences, Laura finds empowerment in acknowledging and harnessing the inner resources available to her, ultimately leading her towards a path of greater self-awareness and resilience.

Key Insights

- **Setting Boundaries:** Laura recognized the importance of setting boundaries and not taking on responsibilities that were not hers. Her interaction with Joseph inspired her to distinguish between her obligations and those of others, leading to a greater sense of balance and clarity.

- **Improved Communication:** Laura's visible subconscious played a pivotal role in improving her communication, especially in her interactions with her partner. The voice of reason provided by Joseph helped her refrain from unnecessary confrontations and contributed to more harmonious relationships.

- **Embracing Change and Happiness:** Laura's overall sense of happiness and well-being continued to grow, partly attributed to her connection with Joseph. Her ability to adapt to change and find joy in new experiences was enhanced by her interactions with her visible subconscious.

- **Building Self-Confidence:** Laura expressed a desire to enhance her self-confidence when addressing issues with friends or acquaintances. She acknowledged that she needed to express her feelings honestly and confidently, seeking guidance from Joseph to navigate these situations with more assurance.

- **Alter Ego or Inner Mentor:** Laura's relationship with her visible subconscious resembled having an inner mentor or alter ego. Joseph, in the form of a Dominican-accented figure, served as a source of motivation, wisdom, and tranquility.

Laura's remarkable ability to engage with her visible subconscious in profound ways illuminates the extraordinary nature of her journey. While not everyone may encounter such interactions with their subconscious, engaging in these dialogues often yields intriguing responses. These responses often circumvent certain filters imposed by our conscious minds, presenting us with the choice to either heed their wisdom or not. When we opt to overlook these insights, we forge a unique and valuable learning experience. In essence, this practice trains us to appreciate and ponder the wisdom emanating from our inner guide.

Distinguishing itself from other visible subconscious manifestations, Laura's "visub" possesses a distinctive Dominican accent, adding a unique layer to her journey. Ethan's idea of giving Blue a distinct voice may indeed hold promise and align with the uniqueness of Laura's experience.

While Laura increasingly leans on Joseph for support, she sometimes wonders if there's a broader spectrum of help he could offer. She wrestles with how best to approach these inquiries, which reflects her evolving comprehension and exploration of her visible subconscious.

Stay tuned for the next installment, where Laura's adventure with her visible subconscious takes an unexpected turn, unveiling new dimensions of this fascinating phenomenon.

11

A VISIBLE SUBCONSCIOUS
BECOMES HER

 "When your inner world comes into order, your outer world will come into order."

— I CHING

I s happiness a discovery, or is it a creation? And what about our sense of self—the notion that one is a distinct entity in control of their actions and thoughts? In the documentary *Your Brain: Who's in Control*, Dr. Kasthuri aptly describes the feeling of being a single 'me' as a product of the intricate network of nearly 90 billion neurons, creating the illusion of an individual presence within our minds.[1]

Much of what happens within us converges into a singular awareness we recognize as our "self." In this chapter, we'll explore a unique perspective on happiness and something totally unexpected, especially in the context of Laura's visible subconscious or "visub."

Nearly six months had passed since Laura's initial encounter with Joseph. Joseph is a unique visible representation of her subconscious mind, resembling a dark-skinned Dominican man. What distinguishes Joseph is Laura's ability to summon him at her discretion by calling his name, see him with her eyes shut, and engage in verbal communication with him.

After several weeks without any communication from Laura, I was eager to reconnect with her on the phone. Recently, Laura and her husband began a new chapter by relocating to the East Coast.

With a genuine curiosity to learn more about her experiences with her visible subconscious, affectionately named Joseph, I attentively listened to Laura's voice during our conversation. Her enthusiasm radiated as we conversed. Here's a transcription of the highlights from our phone discussion.

> **PM:** Hola!
> **Laura:** Hi Ponz! How are you?
> **PM:** I'm great! How about you? How was the salon? (Laura sent an SMS before our scheduled check-in time saying that she was still in the salon and would have to call after.)
> **Laura:** Oh my god, Ponz, I've been there for eight hours! (laughing) The hairstylist was new to me. I didn't know where to go to get my hair done since we just moved here. So, I took a chance on this new person. She did a pretty good job, but she was so slow. She mentioned she graduated from school last year and is still learning, so she wasn't quick. My husband just called, like, "You've been gone eight hours!" Oh, my god, I had no idea I was going to be there this long!!
> **PM:** How did it turn out, though?
> **Laura:** I thought it turned out pretty good, it just took forever!
> **PM:** Well, at least it turned out well!

Laura: Yeah, well, I better head home now. I've been gone all day. It's supposed to be my day off, that's why I said you can call me. I thought it would be an easy day, but it just didn't turn out that way. I was stuck in that chair!

PM: (jokingly) I better send your husband a message to warn him to be nice to you.

Laura: (laughing) No, I'm happy with my hair. So, I'm leaving there feeling really, really good, you know. He's probably missed me all day. But it's all good!

PM: Good! How's everything else?

Laura: Oh, Ponz. Life here is just so good! You just feel happy every day here! I can't complain. Really, I can't! I mean, we're still unpacking, but it's been great! My husband's back to work a bit now. He has a subcontracting job, so it's more flexible. It's so much better! So, life is happy here to me. Maybe it's because of having sunshine every day. I mean, I wake up and look out the window, and I literally see palm trees and sunshine outside.

PM: Wow, that sounds awesome!

Laura: The view from my house is beautiful, but I don't have a view of the gulf.

PM: At least you see palm trees and all that. It sounds so relaxing!

Laura: Yeah, it's beautiful! It's a different type of beauty than what I had in Seattle, but I prefer this one. How about you? How are things going?

PM: I'm doing well, managing.

Laura: How's the book going?

PM: I was thinking about our last check-in to conclude the Joseph topic.

Laura: Sure!

PM: A few questions for you. Does Joseph still look the same?

Laura: Ponz, I don't know if he exists anymore; I've been so happy. Unless Joseph just became me, I don't know. (laughing happily) At the beginning, I felt like he was a physical person, but I think he evolved into being a part of me, if that makes any sense.

PM: Yeah, it does.

Laura: And I think Joseph helped me maintain focus. He instilled drive in me. When I wake up in the mornings, I feel focused on being positive rather than unhappy and dwelling on negative. Even when I encounter challenges, I try to find what's good about it. For example, my doctor advised me that to effectively lose weight, I should engage in an hour-long workout. While I haven't reached that hour mark yet, I've progressed to 45 minutes, so I'm focused. I've increased from 30 to 45 minutes! This means I only have to add another 15 minutes instead of feeling upset and thinking I can't do an hour. I know eventually I'll reach my goal.

PM: So, it's a gradual process, and you're maintaining consistency.

Laura: Exactly. I've also noticed that I start my mornings with a workout. Previously, I only listened to gospel music, which I still do, but now I also incorporate positive messages, such as sermons.

I like Joel Osteen. I listen to him a lot. But lately, I've been listening to him almost every morning. I find uplifting messages he's got on YouTube, and start my day with them, which sets a positive tone for the rest of my day. I have joy, and I always find joy. I don't look for, I guess, side events.

Even with my husband, I think our relationship is a lot better because I'm better. I'm not focusing on the nega-

tive and I'm trying to communicate in a more positive way. And I feel like I'm more like who I used to be, versus how I was before I left Seattle.
I can feel like Joseph is like... like me now! Like... he's me!
PM: That's fantastic!
Laura: I mean, ultimately, maybe Joseph was really me, but... separated out.
PM: Yeah, and now you've merged.
Laura: Yeah! I feel like I'm a different person now! In a much better way. I also think just leaving dreary Seattle and the rains, and seeing sunshine every day, makes a difference in my life.
PM: That makes sense. So, since you relocated, have you had any conversations with Joseph, or...?
Laura: Perhaps initially, during the early stages, because the transition itself was quite challenging. So, I think I ended up asking for help, like, "Okay, Joseph, help me get through this!" But now, I've gotten a handle on things. It took time... it took time! It wasn't an overnight process. Yeah, it was perfect! It's been nearly three months since I arrived, and that's where I've progressed to!
PM: That's awesome! Is it okay if you call on him now? I want to know if he still looks the same, sounds the same, or even acts the same.
Laura: I don't know. I think I need to be upset! (laughs heartily)
PM: You can close your eyes and call on him.
Laura: Well, I'm driving; I can't close my eyes (continues to laugh)!
PM: Oh, whoops! Don't do that then!
Laura: No, I can't close my eyes. I'm sure if I need Joseph, I can channel him. It's just right now, I'm going

to get spaced, and I'm okay. I can't close my eyes right now.

PM: Okay, I didn't realize you were driving.

Laura: Yeah, I literally just left the place, and I was like, "Oh my gosh, I got to call Ponz! He's going to think I'm avoiding him!" Which I was while I was getting my hair done. But I'm not getting my hair done anymore.

PM: And Laura, there's one more thing. Would it be alright if I ask for a brief sketch of Joseph's appearance? Then, perhaps you could take a picture with your phone?

Laura: Oh sure thing! I can definitely do that!

Laura attempted to sketch an image of Joseph in her notebook. Afterwards, she snapped a photo of her drawing with her phone and shared it with me.

A sketch of Joseph and the symbols of happiness he represents

Final Thoughts and Conclusion

In this part of Laura's journey, it's as though the fragment of herself that once ushered in unhappiness has naturally come together. She harmoniously fused with her embodiment of happiness, making her feel whole again. With Joseph's guidance and a positive outlook, she has rediscovered her joyful essence, resolved inner conflicts, and enhanced her relationships. While recognizing that this process had served its purpose, Laura remains aware that she can always draw upon this inner resource again in the future, if necessary.

Key Insights

- **Happiness can be discovered and created:** This insight suggests that happiness is not solely dependent on external circumstances but can be found and cultivated within ourselves. By exploring our inner world, nurturing positive emotions, and adopting healthy habits, we can uncover and build our own sources of happiness.
- **Our sense of self is shaped by neural activity:** Our identity and self-concept are intricately linked to the functioning of our neural networks. The way we think, perceive, and experience the world is influenced by the neural activity in our brains. Understanding this connection allows us to work on shaping a more positive and authentic sense of self.
- **Positive thinking leads to transformation:** Positive thinking has the power to bring about significant personal transformation. When we embrace optimistic and constructive thought patterns, we can change our behaviors, perspectives, and ultimately, our lives.
- **External factors influence well-being:** Our well-being is not solely determined by our inner thoughts and feelings; external factors play a crucial role too. These external influences, such as our environment,

relationships, and life circumstances, have a direct impact on our overall well-being.

- **Wholeness through integration:** This key insight emphasizes the importance of inner harmony and self-integration. Acknowledging and reconciling the various aspects of our inner selves leads to personal growth and greater emotional balance.

Laura now embraces her newfound vitality, much like driving a Ferrari at full throttle, all guided by her visible subconscious. Interestingly, Laura's exceptional experience has left us wondering how others might use their metaphorical Ferraris. How are they embracing their renewed vigor? And how are they pursuing their passions?

In the upcoming chapter, we join Sam on his journey as he endeavors to manifest his subconscious into visible form. Sam, raised in a Jewish family, finds himself deeply fascinated by the prospect of making his subconscious visible. He is driven by the desire to reconcile his religious beliefs with the concept of hypnosis for self-improvement.

12

UNWRAPPING BEN: SAM'S ENCOUNTER WITH A VISUB

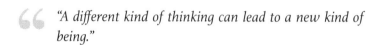 *"A different kind of thinking can lead to a new kind of being."*

— *PONZ MANANTAN*

At a bustling conference during my travels, I serendipitously crossed paths with Sam, a bright individual in his early thirties who sees himself as a late bloomer. Hailing from a Jewish upbringing, Sam found himself entranced by the fascinating realm of the mind and the potential of hypnosis.

As we conversed, the limitless possibilities of hypnosis and the intriguing depths of the mind unfolded before us. Sam, with humility, admitted his limited knowledge on the subject, having only stumbled upon a few articles in the past. However, the notion of revealing the subconscious mind's form enthralled him deeply. This curiosity sparked a series of questions as he sought to reconcile this concept with his religious beliefs.

In December 2022, while visiting Seattle, Sam contacted me, expressing his keenness to experience the visible subconscious. Before commencing our session, I carefully walked him through the process, addressing all his questions and apprehensions.

Within the cozy confines of a room shielded by thick curtains, muffling the sound of freezing Seattle rain, I instructed Sam to get into a comfortable position as I dimmed the lights. Through a series of relaxation exercises and skilled techniques to quiet his critical mind, Sam gradually descended into a state of profound relaxation.

To gauge the depth of Sam's trance, I used the lucidity test. If he can visualize an animal as though it were physically present, he is most probably in a trance state where we could continue our exploration of his visible subconscious. With remarkable clarity, Sam depicted a green and red bird hovering over a flower, merely two feet away. Then, it morphed into an orange tiger, its size no larger than a loaf of bread, completely motionless, and... it was revealed to be a mere stuffed animal.

With Sam now in the optimal state for Bosconization (the process of making one's subconscious representation visible via hypnosis), here's a transcript capturing a riveting segment of his journey.

PM: Describe what you see.
Sam: (eyes closed) I'm not picturing any person, but I have this... it's a visualization of a starburst. Very bright. Floating.
PM: Using your imagination or visualization is totally fine. And as you see the starburst, can you describe the size or any more detail about it?
Sam: It looks to be a couple of feet from me, just

hovering in the air. Very bright! It's like bobbing up and down. And has many points.

PM: Do you like it?

Sam: I don't dislike it.

PM: What impressions are you getting from it?

Sam: Judgment.

PM: Judgment. Can you tell me more about that?

Sam: It's giving me the sense of it being like... a manifestation of something other-worldly. Spiritual. It's just there to observe and watch what I do. And see if it aligns with what it thinks is right or wrong.

PM: Alright, ask it if it's the representation of your subconscious mind.

Sam: Verbally?

PM: Mentally or verbally.

Sam: It's just bobbing.

PM: Is it bobbing just after you asked the question?

Sam: It was before, but now it's moving more, up and down.

PM: Ask it if it means yes when it's bobbing more up and down.

Sam: ... I think it's bobbing even more now.

PM: I see. That means yes if it's bobbing up and down. Now, ask it to do what it means for a "No" answer to a question. What is its way of communication a "No"?

Sam: It's moving in a circle. Like a counterclockwise, facing me, circle.

PM: Alright, so if it moves counterclockwise, it means "No." If it's bobbing up and down, it means "Yes." Could you ask it to come closer to you?

Sam: It did. There's like a hum coming from it.

PM: A hum?

Sam: I didn't notice it before, but now that it's closer, I hear it.

PM: And how does that hum make you feel? Does it make you feel any different?

Sam: A little intimidated. Like it's all-powerful.

PM: Alright, so this starburst is connected to your subconscious mind. Think of it as a representation of your subconscious, and it is part of you. If this starburst does not have a name, give it a name. Or you can ask it first if it has a name, then tell me what it says.

Sam: ... it's bobbing up and down.

PM: Interesting. Now ask what it's called.

Sam: It's still just bobbing, but I feel like I'm holding it now. Like it's settled in my hands.

PM: Great. Now, let's establish communication beyond just movements. Ask it if it can talk to you directly, or send thoughts into your mind. This way, you can immediately get answers to questions that require more than a yes-no answer.

Now ask what its name is again.

Sam: ... I just got the name "Ben."

PM: You got the name "Ben." Did it tell you that? How did it communicate it to you?

Sam: It just appeared in my mind. I didn't hear it.

PM: I see. So, Ben is the name of your subconscious mind. Say hi to Ben.

Sam: Hi, Ben!

PM: What was its response? Did it do anything?

Sam: I just got a sense of like a pulse of energy.

PM: What sort of energy?

Sam: It felt like electricity, buzzing through me.

PM: Interesting. How about we try something fun. Ask Ben to sing a song.

Sam: It's just bobbing.

I attempted to make Sam's subconscious respond better with additional hypnotic suggestions before resuming our conversation.

> **Sam:** It's crackling.
> **PM:** Crackling? Like it's creating a melody?
> **Sam:** It's not recognizable. It's like there are tones, but they seem random.
> **PM:** That's okay.

I've noticed that responses during exercises like this can vary, often reflecting a person's personality and perspective. In Sam's case, it seems like he views his visible subconscious as something serious and dignified. This perspective might restrict his visible subconscious from acting in ways that seem out of character, such as singing a song.

The next test was to see if Sam could command Ben to leave and return at will.

> **PM:** Ask Ben to go away for a bit.
> **Sam:** It flew away.
> **PM:** That's great! Now call Ben back.
> **Sam:** It's back. It dropped out of the sky!
> **PM:** Perfect! So, even though you can't physically see Ben, you know he's there for you. You can always summon him, and he'll be ready to assist you whenever you need. Whether it's questions or guidance, he's there to help.

The next step was to test whether Sam could perceive Ben with his eyes open, so I brought him out of hypnosis.

> **PM:** Hi!

Sam: (looking at PM, appearing more alert) Hi!

PM: Alright, I want you to call Ben.

Sam: Hey, Ben!

PM: (waits expectantly as Sam gazes straight ahead) Can you see him?

Sam: I don't see it vividly.

PM: Where is he approximately from you?

Sam: Like, here (pointing about three feet in front of him).

PM: Is it getting clearer the longer you focus on it?

Sam: Not really, I'm just getting a sense of it.

PM: So, you have a sense that it's right here, but you can't quite make out its appearance, even though you know it's a starburst.

Sam: Yeah, like a ball of energy.

PM: Alright. Sleep!

Sam closed his eyes and returned to a state of relaxation. I offered suggestions to enhance the visibility of the subconscious form when his eyes are open before bringing him out of the trance state.

PM: I want you to call on Ben.

Sam: It's like I don't see it visually, but I feel it. Like I can visualize it in my mind's eye. It's superimposed with my eyes open, like an outline. I can see it moving through the ceiling, swooping down.

This is great progress! With his eyes open, Sam can now perceive it more clearly. Being logical and skeptical, he was attempting to make sense of his experience. After a few more hypnotic suggestions to help him see the form better, we resumed our conversation.

PM: Let's call on Ben again... can you see him?

Sam: Yes, I can.

PM: Good. Now, I want you to think of something you want to work on or improve, maybe a goal or a challenge you're facing.

Sam: (pauses, reflecting)

PM: It can be anything, even if it seems small or something you're already working on.

Sam: ...

PM: Anything?

Sam: Okay, I've got it.

PM: Do you feel comfortable sharing it?

Sam: Yeah. It's about dealing with self-consciousness, letting it control my actions and decisions. Being anxious about how I am perceived and letting that dictate my life.

PM: That's completely understandable. Now, I want you to have a conversation with Ben. Ask him how he can help you with that.

Sam: I just did, and it's flashing.

PM: How did you phrase your request?

Sam: I said, "Make it so that I can be comfortable with myself and not be worried by how I am perceived by others." Is that present tense?

PM: Is it still flashing? What's it doing now?

Sam: It's bobbing.

PM: Alright, that's a yes, it's willing to help. Sometimes, when you ask for something that requires a more detailed response, your subconscious might communicate by sending thoughts directly into your mind. You'll recognize these as coming from your subconscious. Or it might use sounds to convey messages.

Understanding the movements of the visub resembles using a pendulum for guidance. Similar to holding a pendulum still and asking your subconscious to indicate "Yes" and "No" through specific movements—such as swaying back and forth for "Yes" or forwards and backwards for "No"—with the visub, you establish similar signals. Once these signals are set, you can pose questions and interpret the responses. It's as though at its core lies the primal form of communication, similar to binary code—1 for yes and 0 for no.

As the hypnosis session neared its end, I gently guided Sam back into a trance state once more. Before concluding the session and bringing Sam out of this state, I provided positive reinforcements to enhance the beneficial effects of the session.

> **PM:** ... At the count of five, you will come back into your waking state, feeling relaxed, maybe happy, and able to call on your subconscious mind anytime you need to. Every day, your connection becomes stronger, and your interaction becomes better.
> One...
> Two... circulation returning, breathing shifting...
> Three... feeling confident in your new discovery, your new friend perhaps? Your visible subconscious mind, Ben...
> Four... starting to come back into the room, and...
> Five! Eyes open, wide awake, wide awake, wide awake!
> And welcome back!

Sam opens his eyes and yawns, appearing relaxed. He then takes a sip from a can of Seltzer on the table.

> **PM:** Call on Ben.
> **Sam:** I see it!

PM: You see it? Is it here? (pointing to the area Sam indicated earlier)

Sam: Almost (pointing a few inches further to my left).

PM: Is it clearer?

Sam: A little bit. It's still somewhat translucent.

PM: That's normal. Translucent is typical.

Sam: Yeah. It's like a hallucination, you know. It's like visualization.

PM: Yes, translucent is how it normally is. Ah, Starburst!

Sam: Yeah! Ball lightning-kind of thing.

PM: Okay, so you said it's right over here (pointing to the area where Ben is). Close your eyes and tell me if you can see it. Or, call on it and see how far it is.

Sam: (closing his eyes) I didn't see it when I closed my eyes. But when I called it, it swooped into my mind's eye.

PM: That's good! In your mind, how far or close is it?

Sam: The same.

PM: And does it look the same? Is the size the same?

Sam: Yes.

PM: Great!

Sam: (opens his eyes and takes a sip of carbonated water. Speaking in a hushed tone) Why "Ben?"

PM: Why "Ben?"

Sam: (still whispering) Such a weird name! Seems so random!

PM: (chuckling)

Sam: Sorry.

PM: It's alright. Well, that's its name!

Sam: I guess. I'm getting a sense that it's not evil, but it doesn't feel friendly.

PM: What do you mean?

Sam: I don't mean unfriendly, but it's like... stern! A stern presence.

PM: If you look into yourself internally, do you see a reflection of a part of yourself in it?

Sam: (contemplating)

PM: Is there a part of you that's somewhat stern in the way you handle things or something like that? Because the subconscious often mirrors aspects of yourself, in my experience.

Sam: I don't think of myself as being strict with myself. I think, for a long time, I've felt that externally. I asked if it's friendly, it started bobbing up and down.

PM: That's a yes.

Sam: Is it always benevolent, in your experience?

PM: Yeah!

Sam: And the same for others and yourself?

PM: Absolutely! I've never encountered anything malevolent. It's like... you. It's there to protect you; it's your subconscious.

Sam: Right. Yeah, I feel it has my best interests in mind. But again, the sternness. Might be because it's not saying much. It's like it's giving me the silent treatment.

PM: For some, communication isn't always through words; it might be more like facial expressions, or it "inserts" thoughts directly into their minds. Others might have verbal exchanges with it, receiving responses in words. There are variations. Sometimes starts with expressions, then progresses to words. Some have experienced it the other way around.

Sam: It evolves.

PM: Right. And sternness does not necessarily mean it's negative.

Sam: Like tough love... this definitely was super relaxing. If nothing else, cool!

In Matt's case, he compared Bosco to his best self, saying that Bosco embodies all his positive traits, as if he's always operating at peak performance. He described Bosco as confident, bold, and radiating a quiet positivity. Although Bosco doesn't emote, he has an undeniable air of happiness and assuredness. Over time, Bosco has evolved, now feeling as solid and resilient as a rock or diamond—a double pyramid in this case, reflecting its further development.

Ben appeared a little subdued, making me wonder if he shared some of the capabilities of the other visubs. It was time to put Ben to the test, so I explained to Sam that I planned to pinch his leg to establish a baseline for pain sensation and demonstrate the effectiveness of his visible subconscious in pain management. Sam agreed, and as I pinched his upper leg, a vivid memory rushed back to me of instinctively turning my eyes away as a nurse prepared to administer my COVID-19 shot.

After the pinch, Sam acknowledged feeling some pain. Now, the success of this demonstration rested on Ben. Would he be able to perform like the others, or would he prove to be the exception?

> **PM:** Call on Ben.
> **Sam:** Ben!
> **PM:** Tell Ben to numb this area (drawing a circle about 4 inches in diameter on Sam's upper leg) so it won't feel any pain.
> **Sam:** Ben, numb this area (re-drawing the circle on his leg with his right index finger) so I won't feel any pain in it.
> **PM:** What did it say?
> **Sam:** Ready.
> **PM:** Alright (waiting for a few seconds before pinching the area within the imaginary circle).

Sam: (takes a sip of water as I pinch him a second time, keeping his eyes on the can he was holding) How hard are you pinching?

PM: Harder than before.

Sam: (deciding to watch as I'm about to pinch him again, he jerks his leg away just as I pinch it) Ouch!

PM: (startled) Sorry!

Sam: Oh. Well, it just looked painful! (laughing) It didn't feel painful!

PM: (couldn't help but laugh at Sam's puzzled expression) I was pinching it harder than the first one!

Sam: (Looking at me in disbelief and chuckling briefly)

PM: How about here? (pinching another area of the leg, about two inches away from the last pinch)

Sam: No.

PM: (pinching just outside of the numbed boundary)

Sam: (eyes widening like he's seen a ghost) Okay, that hurt! (laughing)

PM: Sorry. Alright, now ask him to remove the numbness in this area (draws the area with his index finger). Make it feel back to normal.

Sam: Okay, Ben! Remove the numbness in this area. Make it feel back to normal... okay, that was a yes.

PM: Alright. I'll just give it a few more seconds...

Sam: (getting pinched in the middle of that area) AAAH! (looking surprised at the pain and bursting out laughing) It's trippy! You did the same thing before and after?

PM: Yeah! And this was't even as hard as before!

Sam: (staring at me in disbelief) This shit works! Did you spike my Seltzer?

PM: No!

Sam: Wow! That's wild!

PM: It can also help you relax further. Some people use it as an alarm.

Sam: Calling on your subconscious to wake you up?

PM: Yeah. For instance, someone wanted to wake up at a specific time to exercise. Even before her alarm went off, she woke up. She said it felt like she could hear her subconscious saying, "Time to wake up!"

Sam: That's incredible.

PM: And she's not the only one who's had that experience—asking the visible subconscious and waking up before the alarm goes off.

Sam: So, it is always awake even when you're asleep!

PM: Exactly! So just keep exploring its capabilities.

Sam: I'll give it a shot. It's weird; I'm still a bit cynical even though I experienced it! (laughs briefly)

Sam embarked on a journey into his past life through a brief regression session, uncovering hidden memories that transported him to a serene island. Amidst this idyllic existence, he reveled in the harmonious blend of land and water, immersing himself in breathtaking views and unburdened peace of mind. Recollections drew him to joyous gatherings around crackling bonfires under the shimmering night sky. Interestingly, Sam's present life mirrors this simplicity and avoidance of confrontations, embodying the tranquil essence of his past experiences.

As with Sam's struggles with self-consciousness and low self-esteem, I guided his mind to pinpoint a time, present or past, where these issues originated. He said he could see nothing but got the feeling of being not good enough. A subsequent attempt to recall yielded the same response. To my surprise, Sam mentioned he could see his visible subconscious, something that was totally unexpected. I seized the opportunity and instructed him to request Ben's help in revisiting a moment from his present or past life tied to his self-confidence issues.

This guidance led Sam to recall being in school at around seven or eight years old. He said the memories flowed in snippets: classroom moments, playtime in the yard, feeling out of place both academically and athletically, and a constant struggle to belong. Shortly after this brief journey into his past, I gently eased him out of trance.

In a playful twist at the session's end, which I nearly overlooked, I asked Sam to smell his drink and identify the flavor. "Grape," he replied confidently. On a whim, I suggested he ask Ben to momentarily dull his ability to discern the scent. Sam's facial expression was priceless when the grape smell faded to almost nothing. For the ultimate act, I instructed him to have Ben restore his sense of smell. Sam's amazement was evident when the unmistakable scent of grapes returned!

Final Thoughts and Conclusion

Sam's encounter with his visible subconscious named Ben offers a fascinating glimpse into the world of hypnosis and the potential of the human mind. Throughout this chapter, we witnessed the unfolding of Sam's journey as he explored the depths of his subconscious, and in doing so, he discovered a powerful ally within himself.

Key Insights

- The visible subconscious, represented by Ben, can take various forms and communicate with individuals in different ways. It may use movements, thoughts, expressions, or even words to convey its messages.

- While the visible subconscious may appear stern or serious to some individuals, it is ultimately a part of oneself, created by a higher power, and is there to protect and guide. It may also display some of the person's characteristics.
- Interaction with the visible subconscious can evolve over time, and individuals may experience changes in its appearance, communication methods, and capabilities.
- The visible subconscious can be a valuable tool for various purposes, including pain management, motivation, guidance, and self-improvement. It can also assist with memory recall and even act as an internal alarm clock.
- The visible subconscious has the potential to guide and direct us while we're in a meditative state.
- With practice and belief, individuals can tap into the real power of the visible subconscious.

In the upcoming chapter, we'll explore further into Sam's captivating journey as he navigates the intersection of spirituality, hypnosis, and the mysterious realm of his visible subconscious in pursuit of personal growth. Now armed with the knowledge of how to summon his visible subconscious and harness its power effectively, Sam faces a multitude of possibilities. Will he delve into the depths of his subconscious to overcome lingering self-doubt and unlock his true potential? Or perhaps he'll embark on new avenues of self-exploration to confront challenges and embrace growth. Join us as we accompany Sam on his quest for self-discovery and transformation. Read on!

13

EMBRACING THE INNER STRENGTH

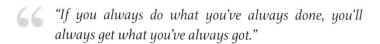 *"If you always do what you've always done, you'll always get what you've always got."*

— *ANONYMOUS*

The mysterious and transformative presence of Sam's visible subconscious, Ben, continues to shape his daily experiences, nudging him toward healthier choices and offering solace in moments of uncertainty. As Sam looks further into this extraordinary connection, he finds himself pondering the nature of his subconscious and the potential for leveraging its influence for personal enrichment.

Within these pages, Sam explores his evolving bond with Ben, contemplating the existence of a spiritual realm while grappling with the fear of embracing his own inner power. Through snippets of chat exchanges and casual updates, readers are invited to witness the profound possibilities nestled within their own inner landscapes.

Follow along as Sam unravels the intricacies of this unique phenomenon and learns to trust in the boundless power within. Our text conversation begins as he takes a stroll along a trail near a serene lake.

December 12, 2022

> PM
>
> How's Ben?

SAM

Chilling. He/It popped into my field of view once or twice today unprompted. Do you ever experience that?

> PM
>
> Some people encounter that when they're preoccupied with something. It's a reminder that Ben is there, ready to assist with whatever's on your mind at the time. Were you focused on anything specific before it happened?

SAM

Hmm. I probably was, but I can't recall anything specific now. Good to know, though. I'll try to be more mindful of my thoughts if it happens again.

> PM
>
> Cool! If you're not comfortable with Ben doing that, it will stop. It evolves alongside you.

SAM

I didn't find it bothersome. It was more like, "Oh, hi! What brings you here?" I don't mind the company! Lol.

> PM
>
> Perhaps you needed company at the time; hence it popped up?

SAM

That's definitely possible.

PM

You're in the woods. A magical starburst ball of energy appears in front of you. You say hi to it... framing it like that sounds like a scene from a paranormal or enchanted tale!

SAM

Lol. It's the next installment of The Adventures of Sam and Ben!

PM

Indeed! Did you engage in a bit of dialogue with it?

SAM

I didn't really have a conversation with it. I guess I still kind of have preconceived biases, indoctrination, skepticism, cynicism, whatever you want to call it. It still feels weird talking to myself. But truth be told, I do it all the time. However, now I'm actually conversing with something that's not physically present. Or maybe it is, I don't know. Does that make sense? It's kind of weird.

PM

Would it help if you think of it as your higher self? Or view it as a new avenue for exploration? Some people hold beliefs in angels and divine beings, yet they've never encountered one firsthand—at least, most of us haven't. But when we have visible proof of the presence of something, some struggle to acknowledge its very existence.

If you were to encounter an angel, how would you react? Would you doubt its reality even as it stood before you? And if it were to vanish, would you question whether it was truly an angel at all? At what point can you confidently declare that something is real enough for you? In Ben's case, perhaps you could keep poking at it until you find satisfaction. Explore. Experiment. It's a tool to help you. Some people use theirs as a listening ear or a sounding board—a comforting presence, if you will.

SAM

Yeah, I appreciate that insight, thank you. Wise words. I've actually been pondering along those lines. Let me pose this question to you. I guess I'm curious what you think. In general, based on your experiences or those of others, this concept of the visible subconscious—the subconscious—is it an actual entity? Or is it just some way of, I don't know, tricking the human mind into thinking things out in a more rational way or something, or thinking things out in a way that would benefit you the most? I hope I'm articulating my thoughts clearly. I'm curious to know if you believe it as an actual being, or is it just something that your brain is manifesting?

You see, the broader concept of the spiritual world is something I still don't have a clear understanding of or acceptance. Though I guess I'm uncertain where I stand on it. Much of my uncertainty stems from religious influences. So, it's a matter I continue to wrestle with, you know? The whole concept of perceiving something intangible—does it truly exist? Is there any real proof to substantiate the existence of such entities? I don't know. It all falls into that category for me—something to explore, as you aptly put it. Poke it.

PM

It's not a separate entity, but rather a manifestation of the mind, drawing from what's already within you. You've never laid eyes on your brain, but you know it's there. Scientists have dedicated years to unraveling the mysteries of the mind, yet they still don't know how it fully works. They continually gain a better understanding and make new discoveries over time.

We don't have to wait for science to discover everything there is about something before we even believe it. Do you require a comprehensive understanding of everything that happens when you send and receive messages on your phone before you believe that it really works and exists? For most people, they know it works; they see the evidence that something takes place, and that functionality is enough for them to accept it.

SAM

Very true. I guess if it works, why should I care that I don't know exactly *how* it works?

PM

Understanding its workings is valuable. But the thing is, nobody yet has a full understanding of how it works. But perhaps, in another century, scientists will finally exclaim, "Eureka! We've cracked it! We now know how it works!" And thanks to the gracious donation of Sam's brain, they were able to further their studies! 😄

SAM

Ha ha! 😄

December 13, 2022

SAM

How are things there?

PM

Things are busy, but good. How are things with you and Ben?

SAM

Cool, cool. Things are good with us. Lol. He helped me make healthier food choices today.

PM

Really? How? Tell me more!

SAM

Well, I went grocery shopping this afternoon, and I hadn't eaten anything all day, so I was HUNGRY. I realized that leads to me buying all sorts of junk, so I thought, "Hey, let me ask Ben what he thinks I should buy." So, as I shopped, I'd ask him if I should pick up certain items, and it worked like a charm. I ended up with a bag full of healthy choices! Then I thought, "Hmmm... maybe I should swing by McDonald's. It's right next door." But when I checked with Ben, I got a clear vibe of, "Who are you kidding? You don't need a burger. You just got a whole bunch of healthy food. Go home and eat that!"

PM

Nice! 😄 Can you give me an example of how you asked while at the grocery?

SAM

"Hey, Ben. Can you tell me if you think I should get this?" Just like that.

PM

Ah, then he responded with gestures. Awesome! I'm glad you're using it! 😄

SAM

Right. Or he'd give off a "Yeah!" or "Nah…" kind of vibe. Honestly, it still feels a bit odd. There's something about it that makes me uncomfortable, and I haven't quite pinpointed what it is.

I think it's probably just my ingrained skepticism. There's a little voice in my head that sounds like my dad saying, "Come on, do you believe in this subconscious energy mumbo jumbo?" But that's really a side effect. So far, it's just cool that I can use it, and it apparently works!

December 16, 2022

SAM

I wonder why my subconscious did not resemble a human instead. Maybe it could take on that form.

PM

Perhaps you could ask Ben.

SAM

I'm not getting anything.

PM

No answer? No movement? Or is that the equivalent of giving you the eye 😏 Like, "Really, Sam? Are you serious?"

SAM

Lol. Yeah, maybe. It was bobbing slightly. But yeah, it gave off a vibe like, "Come on, you know I can't do that." Although that could have been my own pessimism creeping in.

PM

LOL. Yup! They communicate through vibes, for sure! Similar with some of the other visible subconscious entities. I think the reason you don't perceive a face is to prevent you from feeling judged or something.

SAM

Oh, that's an interesting theory and it makes a lot of sense! Does the appearance of the subconscious ever evolve over time?

PM

Yes, it does.

SAM

So maybe one day I'll see a face. Once I'm secure enough to not feel judged. LOL.

PM

Probably 😄 That's a possibility.

December 17, 2022

Prior to this day, I asked Sam to sketch his visible subconscious, take a picture, and send it to me. Sam shared the graphic image he made below.

Graphic representation of Ben, a glowing ball of energy

PM

How big is it?

SAM

About a foot or foot and a half in diameter. And it's very bright! It has tendrils that extend straight out of it.

PM

How long are the tendrils?

SAM

Approximately an inch or so.

PM

I see. Are the tendrils in motion? How about the entire entity?

SAM

Yeah, they're sort of… wiggling a bit? The whole thing emits an electric crackle, and the light pulses. It seems to bob up and down at least a little continuously.

PM

Nice!

December 18, 2022

PM

You're still awake!

SAM

Indeed, I am!

PM

What are you up to this late?

SAM

Working, believe it or not. I'm in a flow.

PM

Working?!?

SAM

Lol. Yup! But I should probably try to get some sleep. Just a big project that I want to get done ASAP, and I couldn't sleep, so…

PM

Fair enough. Well, Ben? Make it so that Sam goes to bed and gets into a deep state of relaxation and sleep as soon as possible! 😌

SAM

Alright, I guess I'm outvoted.

PM

What did it say?

SAM

It said I should probably go to sleep because it's going to make it hard to function tomorrow. The voice of reason.

PM

There you go! 😄 I should do the same.

December 19, 2022

PM

Heya, Ben! How are you doing?

SAM

Ben is vibing, trying to keep me in check.

PM

Hehe. Tell me more.

SAM

It feels like whenever I'm about to make a questionable decision, Ben shows up and shoots me a look. I'm still getting used to his presence, and I don't always heed his guidance. But it seems on point when I do. Like just now, I was contemplating on grabbing some food, heading home, and unwinding with a smoke. Consulted with Ben, and I'm out for a walk instead.

PM

Cool! Tell me more about how that consultation went.

SAM

I called on Ben and asked if it was a good idea. Got an adamant no, which, I guess, you don't have to be a genius to realize.

PM

And you chose to listen to it this time 😊. Did Ben suggest the walk, or was that your own idea?

SAM

I think it was me. It's something I've been contemplating. Is Ben's response truly the answer of the entity, or is it just common sense? Common sense tells you that getting high in the afternoon isn't the healthiest choice. Much better to go for a walk, right? So yeah, I was kind of debating on those two options in my mind, on my own. Ben wasn't part of the equation until I called upon him.

I suppose it doesn't really matter because I think I've been deifying Ben too much, turning him into some super spiritual or religious entity. I don't think that's how you portrayed it. It's just my interpretation based on what I'm familiar with. I think I need to separate the two —the religious aspect from whatever the subconscious thing suggests. It doesn't really matter, but doesn't have to be God.

PM

I was just trying to understand the entire process 😊. If it works for you, that's what matters. Sometimes we know what's right but still choose otherwise until we receive external validation that we were correct in what we were thinking. It helps.

For me, I used to wrestle with decisions internally, wishing there was a straightforward way to discern or get told the right choice. The visible subconscious aids in this to some extent. It may vary for others.

SAM

Right, that all makes sense! I think I'm overcomplicating things! Lol.

PM

I think this is also a nice creation of God, and we are being creative about it. Is Ben quite luminous? I think it's amazing, being able to see and interact with a sentient-like bright starburst. Kind of from a higher intelligence or something. I want one!!! Lol.

SAM

Ha ha! Yeah, it's almost angelic. A radiant yellow-golden light.

PM

Dang! Lucky you! Why do you think your subconscious chose that form?

SAM

Hmmm… that's a good question. I haven't really thought of it. I'm not sure.

PM

Ask Ben, see what it says.

SAM

Not much, really. It seems to be a representation of something powerful. Perhaps I'm not asking the right way.

PM

Do you think the representation of something powerful resonates with you? That perhaps you would trust it more compared to, say, a pumpkin or scarecrow, which you might dismiss as malevolent, judgmental, or untrustworthy?

SAM

No, if anything, it's the opposite. I have this sense of it being all-powerful and like a deity. Not evil, but not overwhelmingly benevolent either. And I do feel judged. But since it's so powerful, I feel compelled to 'trust' it.

PM

Do you think that setup suits you better?

SAM

I'm not entirely sure. Probably not.

PM

How come?

SAM

I think a kinder representation would be more pleasant than a stern "Do as you're told" vibe.

PM

Do you think you'd be less inclined to follow its guidance if it were kinder rather than stern?

SAM

Hmmm... I think you're right. I need to be told what to do! Lol.

PM

So, it's effective then. I was searching for a rationale behind your subconscious choosing that form/manner as suitable for you 😊

SAM

I suppose, but is that healthy?

PM

Unhealthy in what sense? How does it affect you negatively?

SAM

To have that fear of authority.

PM

If that authority is, for example, God, then I think that fear can be constructive. A certain degree of fear towards authority can be beneficial, as long as it's balanced. Excessive fear can be detrimental. Balance and moderation are key.

And, you'll eventually change the way you perceive and respond to things and situations as you gain more experience and insights. Your interpretation of that sternness may differ in a few months or years. Likewise, your subconscious adapts its appearance and communication style. I've noticed it adjusting over time.

SAM

I hear that. I don't mean specifically God, just any authority figure.

PM

Understood. Have you had the chance to work at various companies under different leadership?

SAM

Nope! My work experience doesn't offer much variety.

PM

I see. You may not have encountered authority figures who abuse their power, practice favoritism, are racist, or exhibit unethical behavior. I wonder if your fear towards these individuals would differ from the fear you currently feel towards authority figures you're acquainted with at present.

SAM

I don't know how much of that I've witnessed firsthand.

PM

As you encounter individuals like that, and as you establish your own values and gain more self-assurance, your perception of authority figures may shift. You might also discern the difference between fear and respect for those in positions of power. Is the fear you experience linked to the prospect of punishment if you do not obey them?

SAM

Perhaps subconsciously? It's hard to say.

PM

Possibly. That's a valid point.

SAM

In most situations, it's not even something where I can get punished. But I suppose it's like I still harbor a childlike fear towards authority figures.

PM

I understand. Interesting! Do you think this is tied to concerns about how others perceive you or the importance you place on their opinions?

SAM

Maybe. I hate conflict and getting in trouble.

PM

How do you typically react when you find yourself in trouble? At least, in your own perception.

SAM

I suppose, nothing, really. It's more of a mental thing.

PM

Reminds me of your past life regression where you inhabited this peaceful island with no worries. Living a simple life, enjoying the waters and nightly bonfires, and the general tranquility. You were a peaceful being.

SAM

I completely forgot about that!

PM

I think it's crucial for you to develop effective mechanisms for managing conflict and disappointments.

SAM

I think I'm getting better at it.

January 4, 2023

SAM

My sleep schedule is a bit off, but I'm trying to get it back on track. It's definitely late.

PM

When you're struggling to fall asleep at night, say something like, "Help me quickly relax, both mentally and physically, so, I can have a restful night's sleep and feel refreshed when I wake up."

SAM

You know, that never even crossed my mind to try! I think you mentioned it during the hypnosis session. I suppose it takes time to get in the habit of using it.

PM

Indeed, it does! The more you realize its effectiveness, the more likely you are to remember it and seek its help.

SAM

Great! Well, thanks for the reminder. I'll give it a shot.

PM

Regarding the relaxation, did you start with "Make it so that…" or "Help me…"?

SAM

"Help me…" I used the wording you suggested. And I think it's working because my eyelids are starting to droop.

PM

Alright, go lie down. It acts fast, I know. Good night. Nighty night, Ben!

SAM

Ha ha! Thank you! Ben went bright like, "YES!!!"

January 21, 2023

PM

The human body is full of wonders! And the fact that Ben can influence the body and its functions makes it even more astounding!

SAM

Absolutely! Last night and tonight, I asked Ben to help in making wise choices regarding vaping—to avoid overindulging. And it really made a difference!

PM

Really? How did it help? Tell me more. Details, please.

SAM

I reached out to Ben and sensed that he was happy to see me. It was like he was in a bouncy, playful mood. I asked him to make it so that I don't get too high, and to minimize the munchies effect, so I wouldn't devour everything in my apartment. And it definitely felt less intense than usual—there were moments when I felt tempted to snack, but then I realized, "Hmmm… I'm actually not hungry, never mind."

PM

That's fantastic! I'm glad to hear that you're using Ben to improve in that area. Regarding not getting too high, is it about experiencing less of the effect, or is it more about reducing the quantity of consumption?

SAM

It's the latter. I aim to be mindful of how much I consume and not just indulge excessively.

I'M REMINDED OF A SITUATION WHEN A WOMAN SOUGHT assistance at the office to gain control over her cannabis consumption. She confessed that she noticed an uptick in her usage whenever she traveled out of state and was determined to break this pattern. After just two hypnosis sessions, she was elated and relieved to have successfully managed to curb her consumption.

Recognizing the issue marks a crucial first step on the path to recovery. When coupled with a strong desire for change, clear goals (knowing what you want), and a well-defined plan and timeframe, achieving such transformations becomes not just imaginable but attainable.

February 3, 2023

PM

Hi Ben!

SAM

Oh, hi there!

PM

How is he? Or it?

SAM

It/ he is good. It's like having a support staff. Helps me make better choices; I feel like I have more willpower than I've ever had!

PM

Really?

SAM

No doubt!

February 12, 2023

PM

Any more interactions with good ole Ben?

SAM

Yeah, we connect every other day or so. I don't think there have been any new kinds of interactions. Just more of the usual assistance with day-to-day stuff and decision-making.

PM

Tell me more. Like what? Can you provide examples?

SAM

Sure, like the kind of stuff we discussed before. For instance, making better choices when I'm shopping. It's like having an extra reserve tank of willpower. That's primarily how I've been utilizing it.

PM

Nice!

SAM

I still feel funny about it but I'm getting used to it.

PM

I understand. Being a sidekick can take getting used to. Having a sidekick does, I mean! 😊

March 7, 2023

PM

I hope you're feeling less stressed.

SAM

Thank you. It comes and goes, but it's okay. Ben helps me deal with it! 😊

PM

How did he help you deal with it? How did you ask him?

SAM

I should take notes, but it goes, "Hey, Ben. What should my next move be? Should I do A or B, etc." And I've noticed that I don't really look for the bobbing anymore. I just get a sense of which to do.

PM

Is it a strong sense of clarity? What is it like? Does he still bob?

SAM

I don't know if I'd call it a strong sense of clarity. Feels more like, "Hey, pssst... here's a hint, go this way." And that's a good question if he still bobs. I'm not sure if he/it (either is fine) stopped, or I just stopped looking for it.

PM

No problem. They evolve, and the way they communicate evolves, too. As for the decisions, were they good ones so far?

SAM

I think so. When I intentionally choose the "wrong" path, I end up regretting it!

PM

That's good to know. Ben is like your good internal voice. The voice of reason, as someone said. Ben's doing a great job of helping/guiding you, and I'm happy to hear that.

SAM

"The voice of reason." Yeah, that's a good way of putting it. Thanks for introducing me to him 😊

PM

You're very welcome! 😊

March 13, 2023

PM

But most of the time, you follow his suggestion, is that correct?

SAM

I'd say 8/10.

PM

Well, have you asked him to change some bad habits or perspectives, if any? "Ben, make it so that..." Asking him what you want directly, being specific, phrasing it in the positive, and maybe including a brief statement as to why/ result if it happened—the benefits to you?

SAM

I haven't, really. As I'm reading this, I'm remembering that you have told me how to phrase stuff like that. And it's like I haven't been using that part of him. It's almost like I don't want to, by limiting him to just being like the friend in the back seat and to just bounce ideas off of versus an entity or something that can change habits and perspectives.

I think subconsciously, it feels like I'm giving him too much power. Does that make sense? Not that I'm afraid of too much power, like he's going to take over. But it's like I'm skeptical of it. So, the skeptic in me is like, "Eh, don't bother to get him to change habits and perspectives and actually modify things. Because that would be acknowledging that it's legit." Versus just having a friend in the back seat to bounce ideas off, which is a lot more agreeable to the skeptic in me. Does that make sense?

PM

So, there is that fear in you. Fear that is keeping you from becoming the best version of yourself. Fear of the unknown. Fear of getting out of your comfort zone or expanding it. If it's purely skepticism, it's not believing something but trying something out to see its validity. More like seeing for oneself if something would work or not. Having that fear of not wanting to give it a shot because you're afraid of what you might discover (and might discover that you were wrong) may be different.

Saying that you're somehow giving Ben too much power is like saying you are afraid to discover that you have a lot of power in you. Because Ben is the same as you, it is a part of you. It is simply a tool in your mind that gives you the key, the more direct access to that power you already have inside of you. When you sleep and dream, you normally have no control over that dream or the random thoughts that pop up in your mind all day.

The mind is a powerful tool. The mind automatically regulates your heartbeat, the movement of oxygen inside of you, the workings of your muscles, and each cell of the body...how much power does it already have?

The scary thing is you currently have little power over much of whatever is happening inside your body and mind. They are on automatic! If negative habits and perspectives are in there, causing you some fear and negative views about some things and situations (sometimes without you realizing why, and you have less control or power to change it), that is even scarier!

Ben is just standing (or floating) there, awaiting your command. Because it can override and re-program what you want changed to make yourself function even better. All you have to do is ask. Give your own self a chance. YOU have the power now, as compared to others who don't have a Ben to assist them.

SAM

So fragile.

PM

Indeed! That's why we have the option to create the future we want and make it so. Because it's not set in stone!

SAM'S LIFE HAS LARGELY REVOLVED AROUND HIS JEWISH FAMILY and the practice of Jewish teachings. However, as he ventures beyond the boundaries of his familiar world, it becomes almost instinctual for him to measure new experiences against the backdrop of his established knowledge. The human brain typically leans towards the known and the "safe." It's perfectly normal to feel a sense of apprehension when stepping out of one's comfort zone; the fear of the unknown is a common companion in such journeys.

In Sam's case, he's currently grappling with this very human reaction because Ben represents a novel concept that challenges much of what he has known throughout his life. This inner conflict and hesitation arise because he finds himself in uncharted territory, facing something unfamiliar. It's entirely reasonable for someone in his shoes to wrestle with these emotions and ponder whether this fresh path contradicts their previous beliefs. There's a compelling temptation and natural inclination to adhere to the safer option—to steer clear of what's unfamiliar. I playfully called him "Sam, the doubting Thomas," always needing a little extra proof before he's convinced.

Have you ever come across something that left you in a state of disbelief, lingering for minutes, hours, or even days? This reaction often stems from the mind's struggle to reconcile new information with what it already knows. It's like your mind is engaged in a tug-of-war with the inconsistency, simply because it doesn't seamlessly fit into your preexisting framework of understanding. Yet, once you summon the courage to push through that initial fear and embrace the discomfort, that's when growth truly begins to take root.

April 13, 2023

SAM

I still have to remind myself of his existence, but when I do remember, I'm quicker to make use of him. It feels more automatic for things like managing discomfort, whether physical or emotional, making better choices, and managing interactions with family. Stuff like that.

PM

Could you share an example of managing interactions within your family?

SAM

Sure, let me paint a scenario. Sometimes, my nieces and nephews can push my buttons with their antics or childish remarks. I used to react strongly, feeling irked by their behavior. But then I realized, they're just kids being kids. We were all there once. Besides, they're not my responsibility to discipline. So, I asked Ben to help me reframe my perspective, to see them as the innocent little souls they truly are.

PM

That's insightful. How effective has that been?

SAM

Remarkably effective! It rarely bothers me now, and if it does, I swiftly remind myself why it shouldn't and regain my composure.

PM

Can you give an example of managing discomfort?

SAM

Well, I guess insecurity has been a big one lately, so I get Ben to lower that feeling. Sometimes it works better than others, but it usually brings some relief, even if temporary.

PM

Perhaps next time, you could articulate the rationale behind your request to Ben, so your system knows the reason it should keep the insecurity feeling low. Adjusting the core programming rather than just treating the symptoms.

SAM

That's a valid point. So, I don't remember how we got on the topic, but my brother was saying they had a guest who claimed to be a hypnotist (trained by one of the top names in Australia, funnily enough.) My brother was saying how the whole thing is nonsense, etc. And someone else at the table chimed in, "Yeah, it's all made up," that she had even once gone for past life regression hypnosis, and it did nothing. Just the typical skepticism I've been absorbing since forever! Lol.

PM

I wonder if it's the same hypnotist I trained under, perhaps Gordon?

SAM

That was my immediate thought, too. Maybe it's the same Australian guy.

PM

Quite amusing, considering you were sitting there, with a visible subconscious. A living testament to the efficacy of hypnosis!

SAM

Yeah, I couldn't help but chuckle silently. I said nothing.

PM

They had no idea that the person beside them had experienced successful past life regression and could effortlessly engage with his visible subconscious.

SAM

Indeed, it's ironic! I was thinking that as well! Not too long ago, I totally would have joined in the bashing despite lacking firsthand experience. That's just what we do. Now, things are opening up a little, right? It's a positive shift.

April 20, 2023

SAM

What would be a positive response?

PM

How about something like, "Ben, make it so that whenever someone comments about me, I feel fine, my body and mind feel at ease, and I automatically ignore the comments. Because I know myself better than anyone else, and I know I am good, kind, and unique!"

Vary it up. The key is to communicate how you want to react to situations, in the present tense, the impact on you, and why you should react that way. By providing justification, you're reprogramming your subconscious to respond positively when faced with the same triggers. Without the rationale, your subconscious might eventually stop responding in that manner because it doesn't have a compelling reason why it should.

Perhaps you can achieve quicker results by helping yourself using Ben. It's like mastering how to use a tool. Like knowing how to create formulas in Excel. Sometimes you want to tweak it a bit to get the desired outcome.

> Dang, who else has the luxury of having a glowing ball of light to assist in making positive changes and actually receive responses? Without their own Ben, others might repeat their requests endlessly without seeing results!

Sam: 😄 I know, it's no small feat. Thanks for gifting him to me!

SOME OF MY CONVERSATIONS WITH SAM REMIND ME OF A discussion I had with a Christian friend about the visible subconscious, where I shared Matt's experiences. When I asked if he was interested in volunteering, he expressed concern, asking, "Isn't that considered evil?" This reaction is quite common when encountering something unfamiliar or not fully understood. Initially, there's a sense of caution until we become acquainted with it, confirm that it's safe, and aligns with our internal experiences and beliefs. In the context of the visible subconscious, it's crucial to clarify that we're not delving into the realm of summoning spiritual entities or elemental beings. Instead, we're nurturing, fostering creativity, and tapping into the resource inherent within ourselves.

Final Thoughts and Conclusion

In this chapter, we ventured into the depths of the human mind, guided by the mysterious presence of Sam's visible subconscious, known as Ben. As we conclude our exploration, it becomes abundantly clear that the visible subconscious is a wellspring of untapped potential, capable of guiding, empowering, and transforming our lives in profound ways.

Key Insights

- **The Power of Self-Direction:** Sam's interactions with Ben highlight the incredible power of self-directed change. By simply asking, Sam can initiate shifts in his thought patterns, behaviors, and emotional responses.
- **Balancing Skepticism and Faith:** We witnessed Sam's initial skepticism and eventual acceptance of Ben as a trusted ally. His journey serves as a reminder that it's natural to question the unfamiliar, and embracing new possibilities can lead to personal growth.
- **Harnessing Inner Resources:** Ben is not an external force but an inner resource within Sam. This realization opens doors to a world of potential for each of us to tap into our own visible subconscious and effect positive change.
- **Transforming Perceptions:** Sam's ability to alter his perception of family interactions and manage discomfort showcases the visible subconscious' capacity to reshape our outlook and responses to life's challenges.
- **Overcoming Fear:** Like Sam, we may initially fear the unknown. However, as we confront our apprehensions and push beyond our comfort zones, we unlock the true potential of our visible subconscious.
- **Adaptability:** The visible subconscious evolves alongside our understanding and utilization. It can adapt to address specific needs and desires.
- **Programming Change:** By using clear, positive, and justified requests, we can program our subconscious mind to modify deeply ingrained habits, beliefs, and perspectives though the visible subconscious.

In the upcoming chapter, prepare to be enthralled by more mesmerizing tales and see the remarkable ways individuals are tapping into their visible subconscious!

14

REAL-LIFE APPLICATIONS: TACKLING CHALLENGES WITH THE VISIBLE SUBCONSCIOUS

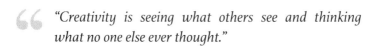 *"Creativity is seeing what others see and thinking what no one else ever thought."*

— *ALBERT EINSTEIN*

In the following pages, you will discover a collection of firsthand accounts from individuals who have harnessed the power of their visible subconscious in various aspects of their lives. These narratives offer a glimpse into the immense potential of engaging with a visible subconscious.

While some stories you're about to read may seem extraordinary, it is essential to recognize the growing acknowledgment of the importance of the subconscious mind, supported by extensive research in the field.

For instance, in the medical field, Tomell (2009) authored an article titled "Subconscious Relief: Hypnosis Gains Acceptance as Medical Treatment." This piece explores the incorporation of hypnosis, a method for tapping into the power of the subconscious mind, as a vital component in the care of cancer patients.[1]

Notably, the visible subconscious can evoke effects that can parallel those experienced during hypnosis, highlighting its potential as a therapeutic tool in medicine. This recognition underscores the profound impact that accessing the visible subconscious may have on medical treatments and patient outcomes.

Truly, the only limits are those of creativity and imagination!

Blood Draw

A PARTICIPANT RECENTLY SHARED AN INTRIGUING EXPERIENCE with drawing blood for a home test kit. The kit required pricking the finger and collecting several drops in a vial until reaching a specified mark. Initially, he pricked his left ring finger. However, after a few drops, no more blood would emerge, even after the continuous massaging of the lower end of the finger. Tests like this requires pricking the same finger on the other hand as needed, so he attempted the same procedure on his right ring finger, hoping to fill the vial, but encountered the same issue—it stopped producing blood after a few drops. Despite squeezing and massaging the finger diligently, he couldn't get the remaining drops needed.

With no other ring fingers left to prick, he reluctantly considered pricking the same finger a second time, though he detested the idea. But then, he recalled his visub. He requested help from his visible subconscious, asking for the blood to flow easily from the wound so he could get the last few drops to fill the vial.

After about 10 seconds of making the request, he gently squeezed the finger, and to his surprise, a drop of blood effortlessly welled out of the wound. He expressed gratitude for the help and massaged the finger slightly, causing three more drops to emerge with ease. Once he had filled the vial, he requested his visub to stop the flow of blood, and he carefully wiped his finger clean.

Curiously, when he tried massaging his left finger, it still didn't produce any additional blood as the right one did. Despite not using a band-aid on his right finger, he noted that no more blood came out after the successful help from his visub.

Driving and Anxiety

EXPERIENCING A TRAUMATIC EVENT CAN TRIGGER HEIGHTENED anxiety in an individual. Involuntary reactions may arise when faced with situations reminiscent of the trauma. One participant, for example, grappled with such challenges. On cold days, driving alone for extended periods would send him into a panic. He would begin to hyperventilate, feel dizziness creeping in, and often needed to pull over to regain his composure. This began to manifest during commutes to certain work sites, to the extent that he began avoiding some of these routes.

Then, one chilly day on the highway, those all-too-familiar sensations returned. Recalling the technique I'd shared with him, he turned to his visible subconscious for support. He requested it to make him feel calm and safe, both body and mind while visualizing himself driving at peace during different phases of his journey: in the present moment, at the journey's midpoint, and upon nearing his destination. Remarkably, within moments, he found himself enveloped in the very tranquility he had pictured. To him, that moment was an enormous relief!

While this strategy didn't eradicate his episodes instantly, it empowered him to handle them effectively. He would, at times, reinforce his request with rationalizations, reminding himself that the traumatic event was well in the past. Over time, these episodes became rarer, and after a few weeks, they ceased entirely.

Feeling Cold in the House

ON A CLOUDY DAY DURING SPRING, CARLOS WAS WORKING FROM home. Around an hour before noon, he felt a noticeable chill in his house. He wanted to avoid wearing a jacket for the sake of mobility, but the cold was hard to ignore. He went to a different spot in his house, but the chill seemed to follow. Hoping to adjust naturally, he sat still for a moment, but the cold continued.

Carlos then had a thought: could his visible subconscious help him feel warmer? If it didn't work, he always had the backup option of wearing a jacket. So, he asked his visub to make it so that he felt warm and comfortable. Just a few seconds after making the request, he noticed feeling an odd sensation near his chest. Nothing changed with the cold, and he continued counting the passing seconds in his head. However, after a minute, the coldness faded. While not feeling outright warmth, Carlos no longer felt the biting chill. He stood up and waved his arms around to check. His body had notably adapted to the cooler environment.

Grateful and mildly astonished, Carlos expressed his appreciation for his visub. This minor change made all the difference, allowing him to work with no jacket until lunchtime.

Food Choices and Exercise

IN LATE AUGUST 2022, MATT APPROACHED ME, SEEKING HYPNOSIS for better food choices. I asked if he already sought his visub's help. He hadn't. Recommending an alternative approach, I suggested he ask Bosco first and observe the outcomes. A week later, our conversation continued.

> **Matt:** I've been having those prepped meals for lunch. I tried out a meal prep program and opted for the calorie-conscious option. The meals are pretty nutritious, curated by a chef, clocked in at 500 calories each, which leaves me feeling satisfied.
> Each of the meals is 500 calories, so it's under-filling. I start my day with sweet tea made with Splenda and have it again at lunch. Surprisingly, I found myself skipping snacks around 11:00 a.m.
> I asked Bosco to still help me not get hungry, and it's been great! My appetite feels balanced, and I eat when I need to without feeling overly hungry. I portion my dinner appropriately and find I don't need snacks in the evening. I stuck to this routine for a week, and I can tell there's been a noticeable difference this week as compared to last week. I think it's Bosco's help.
> **PM:** The previous week, you didn't seek Bosco's help when you were struggling.
> **Matt:** Yep!
> **PM:** How did you word your request to Bosco?

Matt: I think I just asked him, "Stop me feeling hungry between meals, and remind me to do exercise." So, I found I tried to exercise at the same time and schedule, and I'll remember. What I remember is Bosco telling me to do my exercise.

PM: Interesting! How does that work?

Matt: It's like if I'm, "Oh, yeah, I need to do a thing," right? But it's like Bosco pops into my head reminding me, and I go, "Oh, hi, Bosco! What is it? Oh, right, the exercise!"

PM: That's neat!

Matt: It's that same, "Oh, yeah, I remember to do the thing" mechanism, but that initially isn't like the remembering of the thing. It's Bosco popping in, and then he says..."

PM: That's awesome! Thanks for sharing!

Matt: No problem! Because we talked about it last week.

Guessing Game

IN THE SECOND WEEK OF AUGUST 2023, CARLOS ATTENDED A conference where he stumbled upon a vendor booth featuring two clear plastic jars. One jar was filled with business cards and folded papers bearing names, while the other held poker chips. It was a twist on the classic Jelly Bean Guessing Game, using poker chips instead.

Noticing no prizes displayed, Carlos decided to join the game just for fun. He entertained the idea of tapping into his visible subconscious to help guess the number of chips but remained skeptical. Just for the fun of it, he called his visub. While looking at the container, he asked his visub to have a good look and feel of all the chips and the space it occupies, and to give a good guess as to how many were there.

Though winning wasn't his goal, Carlos suddenly had the thought of "around 190 to 200, but definitely less than 200" pop into his mind. Uncertain if it was him imagining it, he decided to go along with it.

"So, around 190 but less than 200, and now I have to pick a number. Hmmm..." he thought. He said, "Meh," jotted down "197" on the back of his business card and dropped it into the jar of entries.

Around three weeks later, Carlos received an email announcing he won second prize: Apple's latest earbuds. Only two prizes were awarded. Curious, he inquired about the correct number. He learned his guess was off by just four.

Reflecting on the experience, Carlos pondered whether his visible subconscious truly guided him to make the lucky guess. Maybe his intention to guess accurately, rather than win a prize, played a role. Regardless, he was delighted with his new earbuds!

Headaches and COVID-19 Booster Shot Side Effects

On November 24, 2021, the day before Thanksgiving, I struck up a conversation with Matt, curious about his recent encounters with Bosco:

PM

Have you been using him lately?

MATT

A bit. I asked him to lessen the Moderna side effects. I think it worked a bit. I asked him to help suppress my cough, too, and that worked. Made my throat feel warm when I asked that.

PM

Tell me more. What side effects were you feeling at that time, what did you say to Bosco, and how quickly did you notice the change?

MATT

I felt terrible—dizzy, headaches, fever, muscle pain, sore arm. He made my arm hurt less and helped me manage my headache. I asked him to help with both.

PM

Nice! How long before your request took effect?

MATT

Like, right away!

PM

That's wonderful! And what was your cough like before you asked him to suppress it? Did the coughing also stop right away?

MATT

It was tickly, and it went away quickly.

PM

Nice! It looks like Bosco's been helping you a lot! Just wait till Bosco sends you the bill! Ha ha! I'm glad you're utilizing him more!

I think it is amazing! Please tell me the exact words you said to Bosco and what his response was. Bosco sending you the bill for all his services was a joke.

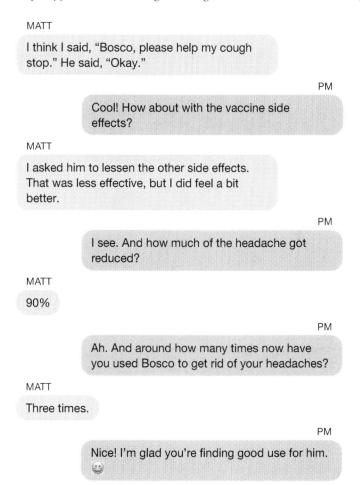

MATT

I think I said, "Bosco, please help my cough stop." He said, "Okay."

PM

Cool! How about with the vaccine side effects?

MATT

I asked him to lessen the other side effects. That was less effective, but I did feel a bit better.

PM

I see. And how much of the headache got reduced?

MATT

90%

PM

Ah. And around how many times now have you used Bosco to get rid of your headaches?

MATT

Three times.

PM

Nice! I'm glad you're finding good use for him. 😄

In subsequent discussions, Matt disclosed his experiences with intermittent headaches, characterized by pulsating sensations. Upon requesting Bosco's help to ease this particular type of headache, Matt observed the intensity decreasing with each pulse. Another participant also recounted experiencing rapid relief from headaches by seeking help from their visible subconscious.

Overcoming Fear of Heights

CARLOS, LIKE MANY OF US, ISN'T A FAN OF HEIGHTS. BUT THERE he was, on a trip to Virginia Beach, gazing up at the Cape Henry lighthouse, feeling a mix of excitement and that oh-so-familiar flutter of fear. It was his first time climbing a lighthouse, and the anticipation was palpable. However, the moment he reached the top and beheld the vast view from the glass windows, his excitement plummeted. His legs turned wobbly, and he clutched the metal rail for dear life.

The plan was to bask in the 360-degree beauty, but his fear of heights had other intentions. The sound of the wind howling through the windows at that height didn't help matters, either. It was as if every gust was taunting him, saying, "Hey, you're way too high up here!"

In a somewhat desperate move, Carlos closed his eyes and called upon his visible subconscious. He mentally implored it to instill a sense of safety and calmness within him. Taking a deep breath, he braced himself and opened his eyes once more. This time, something clicked. His mind quieted, his legs steadied, and he managed to move around, taking in the views with a smile. Though the fear still lingered, it felt distant, tucked away at the back of his mind.

Carlos expressed gratitude to his visible subconscious for assisting him in overcoming his fear, if only for that moment, and began his descent back down.

Pain and Needles

MATT WAS NO STRANGER TO BLOOD DRAWS. DURING ONE OF OUR check-ins in late 2021, he recounted an interesting experience from his recent clinic visit for a blood draw, where he tried something new with his visub.

"Tell me about the time when you used Bosco during your vaccination/medical test," I asked.

Matt eagerly shared his story, "I went for a medical test. I'm not usually bothered by needles and all, but there's always that slight pinch when they draw blood. So, I asked Bosco to make it painless, and then that worked! There was just a warm sensation, kind of like with my hand. Just a really warm sensation where they stuck the needle."

Curious to know more, I inquired, "Where did they stick the needle?"

Matt pointed to his left bicep, near the elbow bend, and explained, "Right there, where the vein is. It wasn't like an IV (Intravenous). But they stuck the needle in, attached the sample bottle on the other end, and swapped it for the next one."

I followed up, "So, the warm sensation made the whole process painless for you, even after?"

"Right," Matt affirmed.

Picking Lottery Numbers

THE IDEA OF ASKING THE VISIBLE SUBCONSCIOUS FOR WINNING lottery numbers may have crossed the minds of several, including Matt. Intrigued by the idea, Matt entertained this thought and decided to ask Bosco for the elusive numbers. However, Bosco's response was unexpected yet insightful. Instead of handing over the numbers, Bosco offered two simple words: "Work harder!" This response could be interpreted as a gentle nudge to prioritize personal effort and dedication instead of relying solely on luck or external windfalls like lottery winnings.

Additionally, Bosco pointed out the potential profitability of real estate. This advice, imparted in early 2021, suggested that exploring real estate investments and ventures might present a more practical and achievable route to financial success.

In essence, Bosco's response aimed to redirect Matt's focus toward hard work, resilience, and strategic investments as the keys to attaining his financial aspirations, rather than banking solely on chance.

Plane and Turbulence

IN SEPTEMBER 2023, CARLOS WAS ON A FLIGHT FROM THE WEST Coast to the East Coast, only to encounter unexpected flight cancellations due to inclement weather. As he approached his destination, the turbulence intensified, causing discomfort and anxiety to surge within him. Desperate for solace, he tightly gripped the seat in front of him, attempting to calm his mind to no avail.

In his distress, Carlos remembered his visible subconscious. With a sense of urgency, he implored, "Make it so that I feel safe on this plane until I reach my destination." Realizing the need for justification, he quickly added, "Because planes are statistically safe modes of transportation." He admitted that it was a spontaneous plea, the first rationalization that crossed his mind.

After a few moments, Carlos experienced a noticeable shift in his demeanor. A profound sense of calm washed over him, dispelling the earlier fear that had gripped him. Despite the continued turbulence, he relinquished his grip on the seat, baffled by the sudden transformation in his emotions. He thought, "What just happened?" As the plane safely touched down, he couldn't help but reflect on the extraordinary experience he had just encountered—a moment of remarkable relief amidst turbulent skies.

Relaxation and Sleep

WHILE EN ROUTE TO HIS VACATION, ANOTHER PARTICIPANT FOUND himself with three hours to spare during his flight. Despite not having a full night's rest, he felt surprisingly alert. Nevertheless, he acknowledged the importance of getting some sleep to ensure he was energized upon reaching his destination.

As he settled into his seat, he made an effort to unwind. Closing his eyes and taking several deep breaths, he focused on calming his body. Then, a thought occurred to him: why not seek the help of his visible subconscious? Silently reaching out, he mentally requested assistance in achieving complete relaxation of his mind and body, hoping it would facilitate sleep.

To his amazement, within about 10 seconds, he noticed a significant shift. His shoulders, which he had assumed were already relaxed, dropped even further, deepening his sense of tranquility. The sudden change was so pronounced that he almost opened his eyes in astonishment!

His first encounter using his visible subconscious for relaxation left a lasting impression, and he knew it wouldn't be his last!

Soothing Itchy Throat

IN A SEPARATE INCIDENT, ANOTHER INDIVIDUAL ENCOUNTERED A mildly itchy throat. Despite repeatedly clearing his throat to ease the discomfort, the itch persisted. Recalling Matt's previous account of using his visible subconscious for relief, this person decided to give it a try.

He reached out to his visible subconscious, asking for assistance in soothing his throat so he could breathe comfortably. Almost immediately after making the request, he noticed a peculiar sensation in his throat. To his amazement, the itch began to fade. Within a minute, the discomfort vanished entirely.

To confirm the relief, he cleared his throat once more, only to find that the itch had indeed disappeared. Grateful for the swift and effective aid provided by his visible subconscious, he felt a sense of relief and appreciation.

Stomach Acid

A PARTICIPANT SHARED A REMARKABLE EXPERIENCE CONCERNING his medication. He recounted feeling an acidic sensation in his stomach occasionally as a side effect of it. To manage this discomfort, he kept antacids in his car. However, one day, caught without any, he found himself facing the familiar burn without relief.

Thinking on his feet, he turned to his visible subconscious for assistance. Shortly after reaching out, he felt a gentle warmth enveloping his stomach, indicating an internal shift. Gradually, the acidity subsided, allowing him to drive and continue his journey far more comfortably than before.

Another participant recounted a similar tale. One night, awakened by stomach discomfort around 3 a.m., he realized he had forgotten to buy antacid earlier in the week. Tossing and turning, he struggled to find sleep as the nagging sensation persisted.

Desperate for relief, he thought of his visub. Sending a mental request to neutralize the excess acid in his stomach, he hoped for some comfort to aid his sleep. To his amazement, a distinct sensation emerged in his stomach shortly afterward. Within a minute, the familiar burn vanished, leaving him wide-eyed with astonishment. He never anticipated such swift relief from a mere mental request!

Stopping A Bleeding Wound

A PARTICIPANT DETAILED AN EPISODE INVOLVING A WOUND FROM September 2021. Below is his narrative of the experience:

During a business trip in September 2021, I sustained a minor cut while staying at a hotel. Although not severe, blood was flowing from the wound, prompting me to wash it thoroughly to prevent infection. Lacking a band-aid, I waited for the bleeding to cease, which it seemed to do at first. However, to my dismay, the wound continued to bleed intermittently throughout the day despite my efforts.

Given my non-diabetic status, I puzzled over the persistent bleeding until I recalled taking aspirin the previous night. Speculating that it might be a contributing factor, I grew anxious, imagining worst-case scenarios of blood loss while away from home.

In a moment of inspiration, I decided to seek the help of my visible subconscious, reasoning that it couldn't hurt to try. With this in mind, I reclined on the bed, took several deep breaths, and closed my eyes. I called on my visible subconscious and said something like, "Make it so that my body starts producing a lot of platelets so that the blood on my wound would clot and stop the bleeding, and help it heal as soon as possible."

As I lay there, observing for any sign of change, I suddenly felt a peculiar tingling sensation on my chest which then started coursing through my body, as if countless tiny vibrations enveloped me. Resisting the urge to open my eyes, I remained still, attentively monitoring the experience. After a few minutes, the sensation gradually subsided, leaving me in a state of bewilderment.

Expressing gratitude to my subconscious, I opened my eyes and decided to rest a while longer. Remarkably, when I resumed my activities, I noticed no further bleeding from the wound for the remainder of the day and the following day.

While I was uncertain of the exact mechanism at play, I was certain that when I appealed to my visible subconscious, I felt that strange tingling sensation throughout my body, and coincidentally, my wound ceased bleeding.

Studying for a Test

I REMEMBER MATT MENTIONING BEFORE THAT HE WAS STUDYING for a test. During one of our brief check-ins, he brought up how Bosco was helping him:

> **PM**
>
> Have you used him for anything else? Apart from those that you've told me?

MATT

> Helping me study! He was able to remind me of answers to the civics test.

> **PM**
>
> Tell me more about that instance, please.

MATT

> For the civics test, when I forgot an answer, I asked him to remind me, and he would tell me the answer. It worked fastest when the answer was on the tip of my tongue.

> **PM**
>
> How did he tell you the answer? Any example?

MATT

> He talked the answer to me in my head. "Bosco, remind me how many years a representative is elected for again?" Then he said, "Two." As he said it, it was like I remembered it, like I knew he was right.

> **PM**
>
> So, you called on him mentally, he appeared, you mentally asked him to remind you of the answer, and he gave you the answer—like made you remember. Is that accurate to say? Was the test a written one?

MATT

> I used him while studying, not during the actual test.

Waking Up

IN ONE CHAPTER, LAURA MENTIONED HOW HER VISIBLE subconscious, or visub, played a role in waking her up in the morning. She noted instances where she would awaken even before her alarm sounded, almost as if prompted by her visub signaling it was time to rise. Sam also had a similar experience when he experimented with it.

However, there was one participant among the group who employed their visub in a different manner. He recounted a scenario where, despite the blaring of his regular alarm, he still felt groggy and hesitant to leave his bed. In such moments, with eyes shut, he called upon his visub for assistance. Specifically, he asked his visub to imbue him with a sense of wakefulness, both mentally and physically, with each passing second.

Within a moment, he felt a surge of alertness, and his eyes naturally opened, as if his mind and body had been instantaneously activated. This newfound state of alertness dispelled any inclination to linger in bed, motivating him to promptly begin his day.

Final Thoughts and Conclusion

As we conclude this chapter, we've examined a myriad of real-world scenarios where individuals harnessed the power of their visible subconscious. These stories showcase the incredible potential of engaging with the depths of our minds. We've witnessed how the visible subconscious can serve as a source of support, transformation, and even seemingly extraordinary capabilities.

Key Insights and Visible Subconscious Characteristics

- **Visible Subconscious in Overcoming Anxiety:** Individuals utilized their visible subconscious to alleviate anxiety triggered by traumatic events, driving alone, or fear of heights. By requesting support from their visible subconscious, they managed to regain composure and tackle their fears effectively.
- **Health and Wellness:** Participants experienced relief from physical discomfort such as headaches, stomach acidity, itching throat, and even managed side effects of medical treatments like blood draws and COVID-19 vaccinations by engaging with their visible subconscious. This highlights the potential for using the visible subconscious as a complementary approach to managing health issues.
- **Enhancing Performance and Productivity:** The visible subconscious was harnessed to improve focus, memory recall during studying, and even aid in decision-making related to food choices and exercise routines. By seeking assistance from their visible subconscious, individuals reported better adherence to healthy habits and improved performance.
- **Manifesting Intuitive Insights:** Some individuals sought guidance from their visible subconscious for tasks like guessing game outcomes and finding creative solutions to daily challenges. This demonstrates the role of the visible subconscious in providing intuitive insights and problem-solving strategies.
- **Facilitating Relaxation and Sleep:** Participants utilized their visible subconscious to induce relaxation and improve sleep quality, even in unconventional settings like flights. By making mental requests for

relaxation, individuals experienced a profound sense of calmness and ease, enhancing their overall well-being.

- **Immediate Response:** Many reported experiencing immediate results upon engaging with their visible subconscious, such as the alleviation of physical discomfort or overcoming fears. This instantaneous response reinforces the efficacy and accessibility of the visible subconscious in real-time situations.

- **Diverse Applications:** From mundane tasks like waking up refreshed to more complex challenges like managing anxiety or physical discomfort, the visible subconscious proved versatile in addressing various aspects of daily life. This versatility underscores its potential as a valuable resource for personal development and holistic well-being.

- **Enhanced Creativity:** While not explicitly mentioned in the stories, the creative potential of the visible subconscious is boundless. It can be a wellspring of innovative ideas and solutions when tapped into intentionally.

CONCLUSION

In this concluding chapter, we celebrate the transformative power of the visible subconscious—an intimate and individualized expression of the subconscious mind. Throughout this book, we have explored the extraordinary experiences of individuals who possess the ability to perceive and interact with their visible subconscious. Their experiences have illuminated the profound impact of this phenomenon, guiding them towards self-discovery, empowerment, and the realization of their aspirations.

As we bring this journey to a close, we extend an invitation to our readers to embrace the potential of the visible subconscious and embark on their own voyage of exploration and self-improvement. Just as Eagleman (2011) aptly noted in his book *Incognito: The Secret Lives of the Brain*, understanding oneself in today's context requires acknowledging that the conscious mind occupies only a small fraction of the brain's vast mansion, wielding limited control over our perceived reality.[1] Perhaps envisioning a visible subconscious as a Jarvis-like entity within this metaphorical mansion could further illuminate its role and significance.

The concept of a visible subconscious—where individuals actively engage with their subconscious in a visible form—presents a fascinating realm for exploration. It seems to act as a mediator between the brain's left and right hemispheres, offering subjective insights unique to each person. In today's society, this concept holds great relevance, as it allows us to gain a deeper understanding of ourselves.

In the hypnotic state, we provide the brain with information that shapes a new reality—the reality of the visible subconscious. This personal reality doesn't have to be real for anyone else, and that's where the magic happens. It creates an augmented experience, allowing us to break free from the negative beliefs we've carried and reinforced over the years, allowing us to shift our perspectives, change our emotions, and move into a new state of being. Welcome the change and the discomfort, for they signify growth and expansion to your new normal. Learn to consciously let go of the small stones you have accumulated all these years that have weighed down on you collectively. Travel light, travel strong, and focus on what matters.

While the visible subconscious remains relatively unexplored in therapy, its potential as an additional therapeutic approach holds great promise. Stories shared in these pages provide glimpses into the immense therapeutic possibilities when therapists harness its power. It opens new avenues for understanding and healing, offering a unique and effective means of contacting the subconscious mind and achieving visible results.

You might have observed parallels in the tests conducted with various visible subconscious forms. Despite their unique appearances, similar tasks produced comparable outcomes, suggesting shared capabilities among them.

You might also be curious about the purpose behind requesting the visible subconscious forms to sing. While some reproduced the songs directly in the individual's mind, others vocalized the tunes in the owner's voice. If the visible subconscious can access and play songs from a person's memory, providing an auditory experience similar to hearing them externally, imagine what other remarkable abilities it might possess! This capability also suggests that it can use songs to communicate with a person. Have you ever been pondering something when a part of a song suddenly popped into your mind, and the lyrics contained exactly what you were looking for?

Stay open to the notion that within your mind lie uncharted territories awaiting exploration, where profound insights and guidance can spark transformative changes.

Through the narratives of individuals who possess the visible subconscious, we aim to inspire readers to explore this uncharted territory of self-discovery and self-improvement. May these stories ignite curiosity and open minds to the untapped reservoirs of strength and wisdom within us. Often, the breakthrough you're waiting for is buried in the very effort you're hesitating to make.

Popow (2018) stressed the significance of valuing individuality over conformity, encouraging individuals to trust themselves, nurture creativity, and remain open to opportunities, because it's all about the mindset.[2] Activating the visible subconscious unlocks new channels for communicating with the subconscious mind, expediting the realization of the mental images we harbor—whether positive or negative—pertaining to ourselves or our circumstances.

In practical terms, if negative mental images arise, perhaps fueled by fear or other influences, it's prudent to promptly redirect our thoughts and replace them with positive ones. Failing to do so may inadvertently bring about the very outcomes we feared.

Embrace the power of your own subconscious mind, even if it may not be visible in the same way. Enhance its capabilities through meditation. Trust in its innate wisdom, unlock its potential, and allow it to steer you to a more empowered and enriched life.

This brings to mind the story of Edgar Cayce, a humble Sunday school teacher from Kentucky, whose trance-like states yielded profound insights and prophecies benefitting countless individuals. Despite lacking formal education, Cayce's legacy comprises over 14,000 readings. Even today, scholars, researchers, and spiritual enthusiasts scrutinize, admire, and contemplate his contributions. Cayce believed that others possessed similar abilities, and perhaps the visible subconscious serves as a modern-day conduit to access a piece of that insight within each of us, provided we remain receptive. My visit to his hospital in Virginia Beach in 2023 left me wishing for something similar—a place dedicated to helping others and a sanctuary to furthering my research.

Many of us desire change in our lives, yet we're often unwilling to invest the time or effort to take the first steps. More often than not, we fail to realize that the work we're delaying is the miracle we've been expecting.

The visible subconscious isn't just a concept; it's a call to action. It's about making desired transformations tangible and achieving a higher level of self-improvement. Discover the art of partnering with your subconscious and unlock hidden potentials for your personal transformation. Meet yours, today!

For more information, check out my website at:
www.unsealedminds.com/visible-subconscious

ACKNOWLEDGMENTS

I want to extend my heartfelt gratitude to all my research participants. Your time, candid feedback, and willingness to step outside your comfort zone played a crucial role in shaping this book. A special thanks to Matt for your flexibility and for accommodating the evolving requirements during the research process. Your support made a significant difference.

Thanks to Lia Ocampo, a fellow writer and former co-worker, for sharing her experiences in the realm of book writing and offering words of encouragement along the way.

To my dedicated beta readers, with particular appreciation for Mary Kennedy and Carole Williams, thank you for your sharp eyes in spotting typos and your thoughtful feedback on key parts of the book. Your contributions helped fine-tune this work and were truly appreciated.

And to you, my reader—thank you for joining me on this adventure with an open mind and heart. Your curiosity and willingness to explore new concepts mean more than words can express, and I truly hope this book ignites something meaningful in your life.

APPENDIX A

A Quiz to Determine Your Susceptibility to Hypnosis

Can You Be Hypnotized?

Below is a short quiz consisting of 10 items that can help determine whether you are susceptible to hypnosis. Having a huge hypnotic potential means having the chance to unlock your hidden potential to give you the power to change your life for the better.

For each number, take note of how many points correspond to your answer. At the end of the quiz, add all the numbers up. The scoring guide is below the last question.

1. Have you ever been so engrossed in a book or movie that you lost track of time and your surroundings?

    a. Yes, often (2 points)
    b. Sometimes (1 point)

c. Rarely (0 points)

d. Never (0 points)

2. Can you picture a situation or scene in your mind so clearly that it feels like you're actually there?

a. Yes, easily (2 points)

b. Sometimes (1 point)

c. Rarely (0 points)

d. Never (0 points)

3. Do you ever feel so focused on what someone is saying to you that you don't notice what's happening around you?

a. Yes, often (2 points)

b. Sometimes (1 point)

c. Rarely (0 points)

d. Never (0 points)

4. Can you easily focus on one task/project without distraction?

a. Yes, easily (2 points)

b. Sometimes (1 point)

c. Rarely (0 points)

d. Never (0 points)

5. Would you be able to fully relax and let your guard down around the individual attempting to hypnotize you?

a. Yes, completely (2 points)

b. Somewhat (1 point)

c. Not sure (0 points)

d. No, not at all (0 points)

6. Have you ever felt a big change in your emotions or remembered something clearly because of a taste, scent, or what you saw?

    a. Yes, often (2 points)
    b. Sometimes (1 point)
    c. Rarely (0 points)
    d. Never (0 points)

7. Have you ever daydreamed or zoned out while doing simple tasks like walking, brushing your teeth, or driving?

    a. Yes, often (2 points)
    b. Sometimes (1 point)
    c. Rarely (0 points)
    d. Never (0 points)

8. Are you open to new experiences and willing to try new things?

    a. Yes, very much so (2 points)
    b. Somewhat (1 point)
    c. Not really (0 points)
    d. Not at all (0 points)

9. Do you have a good sense of imagination and creativity?

    a. Yes, very much so (2 points)
    b. Somewhat (1 point)
    c. Not really (0 points)
    d. Not at all (0 points)

252 | *Appendix A*

10. Have you ever been able to get really relaxed or meditate by yourself?

    a. Yes, often (2 points)
    b. Sometimes (1 point)
    c. Rarely (0 points)
    d. Never (0 points)

My Score: _____

Scoring Guide:
0–6 points: Low susceptibility to hypnosis
7–12 points: Moderate susceptibility to hypnosis
13–20 points: High susceptibility to hypnosis

Low Susceptibility to Hypnosis (0–6 points):

If someone lands in this range, it implies they're less prone to the sway of hypnosis. Picture hypnosis as someone attempting to lead you through a dream. In the low susceptibility range, it's as if you're saying, "Nope, I prefer my own dreams, thank you!" Your mind tends to stand its ground, resolutely maintaining control and resisting the hypnotist's attempts to steer your thoughts or perceptions.

Moderate Susceptibility to Hypnosis (7–12 points):

Finding yourself in this middle range is like being easily distracted by background noise. It might take a bit more effort to stay focused, but with the right techniques, you can be influenced. It's similar to being in a daydream, occasionally fully engrossed in the story someone else is narrating, while at other times, drifting back into your own thoughts.

High Susceptibility to Hypnosis (13–20 points):

Scoring in the high range means that your mind is more receptive to the effects of hypnosis. This doesn't imply gullibility; it's more like being a skilled storyteller who doesn't mind letting someone else take the lead of the narrative for a while. It's like sitting around a campfire and immersing yourself in another person's tale—you're open and receptive, and the story can feel remarkably real. Individuals in this range can effortlessly drift into that dreamy state and are more likely to embrace and respond to the hypnotist's suggestions.

Additional Note:

Keep in mind, being susceptible to hypnosis has nothing to do with having a weak will or being easily fooled. It's all about how your mind engages with and reacts to imaginative states and suggestions. Whether you find yourself lower or higher on this scale, it doesn't define your intelligence or strength of character—it simply indicates how you might respond to this unique experience!

Entering a hypnotic state serves as a primary gateway to accessing the visible subconscious within oneself. Individuals who exhibit moderate to high susceptibility to hypnosis generally have greater success in manifesting their visible subconscious forms, among other contributing factors.

However, those with lower susceptibility can enhance their ability to reveal their visible subconscious forms through various practices. These may include dedicating time to relaxation exercises, listening to guided meditation or hypnosis audio files repeatedly, or seeking guidance from a trained hypnotist. Through consistent effort and practice, individuals can increase their likelihood of accessing their visible subconscious manifestations. This journey sets them on a transformative path towards realizing their fullest potential and achieving self-fulfillment. While not everyone may access a visible subconscious, everyone can take strides to foster a deeper connection with their subconscious minds.

APPENDIX B

Exploratory Exercises

Below are exercises on setting goal statements and self-relaxation, which could strengthen your communication with your subconscious mind and the visible subconscious:

- Exercise 1: Proper Goal Setting
- Exercise 2: Self-Hypnosis Exploration
- Exercise 3: Meet Your (Visible) Subconscious
- Exercise 4: Manifest Your Desires
- Exercise 5: Suggestions for New Explorers

Exercise 1: Proper Goal Setting

Let's dive into an exploratory exercise in setting a goal statement and then refining it as a request to better resonate with your subconscious mind. The same concept applies whether you already have a visible subconscious or not. Follow the guidelines below:

- Be specific
- Specify when
- State it positively
- Use the present tense
- Explain how it benefits you

Example 1:

Original Goal: I want to be able to exercise each day.

Revised Goal Statement: (Starting today,) I prioritize exercising for at least 15 minutes daily so that, I feel energized, confident, and well!

Tip: I intentionally placed a pause (comma) before the reasoning statement. Putting a pause emphasizes the statement after it to resonate more effectively with the subconscious mind. It's the equivalent of slipping it the direct message, "I feel energized, confident, and well!"

Request Statement: Make it so that, I exercise for at least 15 minutes daily and, I feel energized, I am confident, and I am well!

Example 2:

Original Goal: I want to learn a new language

Revised Goal Statement: (Starting tomorrow morning,) I practice speaking a new language for at least 30 minutes daily so that, I am fluent, confident, and culturally enriched!

Request Statement: Help me so that, I practice speaking a new language for at least 30 minutes daily and, I am fluent, confident, and culturally enriched!

It is also acceptable to phrase your reasons differently. For larger goals, begin with a manageable and achievable starting point that you can gradually build upon. For example, if your goal is to establish a routine of exercising for 45 minutes per session, start by committing to 15 minutes initially. As you become more comfortable and confident, gradually increase the duration to 30 minutes, then ultimately to 45 minutes. This incremental approach allows for steady progress and ensures successful integration of the desired behavior into your routine over time.

Once you have your goal statement ready, enter a relaxed state, call on your subconscious or visible subconscious, and make your request. Pay attention to any thoughts or feelings you receive. Some people negotiate with their subconscious based on the response or impressions they receive.

Craft your other goals to speak directly to your subconscious, motivating you towards positive action. By setting intentions that speak directly to your subconscious, you also cultivate a mindset primed for success and achievement.

Exercise 2: Self-Hypnosis Exploration

A. Self-Hypnosis: Explore your subconscious with this guided relaxation and self-hypnosis exercise.

1. Find a quiet, comfortable space.
2. Focus on your breathing as you take a few deep breaths.
3. Set your intention to deeply relax, connect with your subconscious, and see your subconscious mind's form.
4. Close your eyes tightly for six seconds, then relax them.
5. Gradually count down from 12 to 1 while visualizing a door to your subconscious. Count with each exhale, and imagine yourself stepping closer to that door with every breath.
6. Once relaxed, imagine opening this door, establishing a direct communication and connection to your subconscious mind.

B. Create Your Subconscious Mentor: Endeavor to create your own subconscious mentor with a name.

1. In a state of deep relaxation as in the previous exercise, focus on your heart area.
2. As you slowly inhale, imagine pulling some of the energy in the form of a white light from your heart area up to the top of your head. As you exhale, allow and feel that energy expanding, covering your entire body. Repeat this process several times.
3. Imagine summoning your visible subconscious mentor by acknowledging it as your inner guide—an influential ally that governs your bodily functions and the workings of your mind. Request that it reveal itself

in a form you can see and interact with. Ask it to communicate through any medium that is convenient —words, gestures, sounds, and so forth.

4. Engage with your mentor by seeking advice or asking questions on a personal matter. Pay attention to any impressions or forms that emerge. Even if you don't immediately see your subconscious form, you might sense its presence. Trust your intuition and heed the insights that come to you.

5. Ask that its presence remain strong with you always. That it would appear and respond whenever you call on it anytime even after the session.

6. As you decide to end the experience, express gratitude before slowly opening your eyes.

By practicing this exercise, you can start to unlock the potential of your own subconscious mind and deepen your connection to it.

Exercise 3: Meet Your (Visible) Subconscious

Cultivate a deeper connection with your inner world through this daily practice. This exercise aims to help you relax, engage with your subconscious, and seek guidance from your inner self.

Follow these steps daily, ideally upon waking up, to cultivate relaxation and familiarity with your inner world. Begin with steps 1 to 4 until your body and mind become accustomed to effortlessly achieving a state of relaxation. Then, proceed with the remaining steps to deepen your connection with your subconscious:

1. Find a quiet, comfortable place to sit or lie down.
2. Focus your gaze just above the horizon level then close your eyes while maintaining that position. This prompts the brain to generate alpha waves, facilitating relaxation and heightened awareness.
3. Set your intention to connect, interact, and see the visible representation of your subconscious mind, your inner guide.
4. Take several deep breaths. Slowly count down from 12 to 1, exhaling with each count. Continue until you reach 1 and feel deeply relaxed. If you find yourself reaching deep relaxation quickly, decrease the initial count as needed.
5. Immerse yourself in that peaceful inner world and become acquainted with that state.
6. Imagine a name for your visible subconscious, like Laura's "Joseph." If another name comes to mind suddenly, feel free to use it instead.
7. Call out to your subconscious with the chosen name, instructing your subconscious mentor to reveal itself

clearly to you in whatever form it desires. You may witness its unique form materialize before you, or you might sense its presence strongly even if you can't see it yet. If nothing appears, imagine it taking a form that resonates with you.

8. Engage in a mental conversation, seek guidance, or simply observe. Pay close attention to any responses, insights, or movements that arise during the interaction. Learn its communication style by asking a few yes-no questions. If you can't yet perceive your subconscious' form or if you sense its presence but it's not yet prominent, you can ask it to move one finger on your hand to indicate a "yes" and another finger on the same hand to mean "no" before you begin asking questions.

9. Request that it always remain with you and make its presence known whenever you call upon it, whether your eyes are open or closed.

10. Express gratitude for its support and slowly open your eyes (you can also count from one to five before opening them).

Open-Eye Interaction: Attempt to interact with your visible subconscious with your eyes open. Call out to it by name and focus on any mental images or sensations that arise, even if you can't see your subconscious' form with your physical eyes. Keep in mind that not everyone can perceive their visible subconscious with their eyes open.

Goal Setting: Ask your subconscious for help with a specific goal. Inquire how it can support you in achieving that goal and listen for guidance.

Remember that accessing and engaging with your visible subconscious may require practice and patience. The more you participate in these exercises, the deeper your connection with this inner resource will grow, increasing the likelihood of encountering its visible form.

Exercise 4: Manifest Your Desires

Harness the power of your subconscious to bring about positive change. Those who can see their subconscious form can skip to step 4.

1. Find a quiet, comfortable space.
2. Close your eyes, take a few deep breaths, and relax.
3. Count down from 12 to 1, knowing that your whole body and mind are relaxing deeper with each count. Breathe deeply, exhaling slowly as you count down until you reach one.
4. Mentally summon your visible subconscious. If you don't have a visible subconscious yet, imagine what yours would look or feel like, envisioning it as a supportive presence, and maintain that image in your mind's eye. Regardless of whether you actively perceive it, your subconscious is attuned to your thoughts and actions.
5. Formulate a clear, positive request for change. Be specific about what you want to achieve.
6. Justify how this change benefits you.
7. Repeat the request in your mind, stating it positively and in the present tense, while visualizing it as already happening. Imagine how it feels.
8. Pay attention to any immediate intuitive insights or emotions that arise. Interact with your subconscious based on these. Individuals with a visible subconscious may perceive quicker responses and have a more interactive experience.
9. Trust that your (visible) subconscious is working to manifest this change (if it said no to your request, work on formulating your request and reason out until it agrees to help).

10. Take a deep breath, hold it for three seconds, and then thank your (visible) subconscious as you slowly exhale.
11. Open your eyes and go about your day with confidence and expectation that positive transformation is underway.
12. Repeat the same steps for another goal, taking time between each.

Exercise 5: Suggestions for New Explorers

1. **Direct Communication:** Practice clear and specific dialogue with your own (visible) subconscious. In a relaxed state, make a focused request related to a personal goal or issue, and observe any direct responses or insights that follow.

2. **Memory Enhancement:** Ask your (visible) subconscious to help you recall something from your past. Close your eyes, relax, and remain open to any flashes of memory or insights that surface.

3. **Stress Reduction:** During moments of stress, enlist your (visible) subconscious to help calm your mind and body. Pay attention to any shifts in your physical or emotional state.

4. **Logical Thinking:** Before tackling complex problems, seek assistance from your (visible) subconscious to enhance your logical thinking and decision-making. Notice any changes in how you approach these challenges.

5. **Exploration of Limitations:** Reflect on the strengths and limitations of your visible subconscious. Identify areas that could be further developed to improve your unique connection and experience.

Discover the power within you and embark on a transformative path of self-discovery with your visible subconscious. Check out the *Additional Resources* page for the audio recording designed to guide you towards relaxation and may facilitate a quicker revelation of your own subconscious form.

As you take on this journey, remember that you hold the keys to unlock your inner potential. Embrace the unknown, trust in the power within you, and witness as your life changes in ways you never thought possible.

ADDITIONAL RESOURCES

Explore the additional resources below to further your understanding and enhance your practice of techniques for bringing out and utilizing the visible subconscious.

Online Training Program for Hypnotists, Allied Health Professionals, and Other Practitioners:
Mastering the Visible Subconscious
This comprehensive package includes a manual, video presentation, session flowchart, and a Visible Subconscious User Guide, outlining a six-step process to facilitate the emergence of a client's visible subconscious during hypnosis. Designed to guide practitioners through each phase of the session, this approach ensures a smooth, effective experience for both the client and the facilitator.

Hypnosis Audio File for Those Wanting to Activate Their Visible Subconscious:
Anthesis: The Visible Subconscious
This audio file is crafted to guide listeners through the process of activating and engaging with their visible subconscious, enhancing the possibility of experiencing it directly. The hypnosis will focus on relaxation, intention setting, and visualization techniques aimed at bringing forth the visible subconscious and tapping into its potential for personal growth and transformation. Visible Subconscious User Guide included.

www.unsealedminds.com/visible-subconscious
www.unsealedminds.com

NOTES

Introduction

1. Emma Young, "Lifting the lid on the unconscious," *New Scientist*, July 25, 2018, https://www.newscientist.com/article/mg23931880-400-lifting-the-lid-on-the-unconscious. Accessed November 28, 2022
2. Mlodinow, Leonard. *Subliminal: How Your Unconscious Mind Rules Your Behavior*. Vintage, 2012.
3. Brian Tracy, "Subconscious Mind Power Explained." *Brian Tracy* (blog), 2021, /understanding-your-subconscious-mind/

1. Unveiling Hypnosis and the Visible Subconscious

1. Yapko, Michael D. *Trancework: An Introduction to the Practice of Clinical Hypnosis* (4th ed.). Routledge, 2012.
2. Weiss, Brian. *Many Lives, Many Masters*. Touchstone, 2012.
3. Gaia. "Missing Links." *Language of the Divine Matrix*. Season 3, Episode 9. Gaia Channel, 2019. Accessed May 5, 2024.
4. Danelek, J. Allan. *The Case For Reincarnation*. Llewellyn Publications, 2010.

2. Peeling the Visible Subconscious Onion

1. Sugrue, Thomas. *There is a River: The Story of Edgar Cayce*. A.R.E. Press, 1997, pp.98-107.
2. Murphy, Joseph. *The Power of Your Subconscious Mind*. Digireads.com Publishing, 2017. eBook.

3. When What Appears, Disappears

1. Thompson, T., Terhune, D., Oram, C., Sharangparni, J., Rouf, R., Solmi, M., Veronese, N., & Stubbs, B. (April 2019). "The effectiveness of hypnosis for pain relief: A systematic review and meta-analysis of 85 controlled experimental trials." *National Library of Medicine*, 99: 298-310. Accessed on PubMed: https://pubmed.ncbi.nlm.nih.gov/30790634/.

4. Matt's Experience: Harnessing the Healing Power Within

1. Talebiazar, N., Choobianzali, B., Hassanpour, A., Goli, R., Shakorzadeh, S., & Ghalandari, M. (April 2022). "The Effect of Hypnotherapy on Hospital Anxiety in Three Children with Cancer: A Case Report." *International Journal of Surgery Case Reports*, 93. Accessed on ScienceDirect: https://www.sciencedirect.com/science/article/pii/S2210261222002073.
2. Speigel, R. B. (Autumn 2011). "The Integration of Heart-Centered Hypnotherapy and Targeted Medical Hypnosis in the Surgical/Emergency Medicine Milieu." *Journal of Heart Centered Therapies*, 14(2). Accessed on Gale Onefile: Health and Medicine: https://go.gale.com/ps/i.do?p=HRCA&u=googlescholar&id=GALE|A303073321&v=2.1&it=r&sid=HRCA&asid=96ed2a6e.
3. Bourmault, N., & Anteby, M. (August 9, 2023). "Rebooting One's Professional Work: The Case of French Anesthesiologists Using Hypnosis." *Sage Journals*, 68(4). Accessed on Sage Journals: https://journals.sagepub.com/doi/full/10.1177/00018392231190300.
4. Dispenza, Joe. *Evolve Your Brain: The Science of Changing Your Mind.* Health Communications Inc., 2008.

5. Testing the Limits: Exploring the Visible Subconscious' Influence

1. Williams, Sarah C.P. "Study Identifies Brain Areas Altered During Hypnotic Trances." July 28, 2016. Accessed on Stanford Medicine: https://med.stanford.edu/news/all-news/2016/07/study-identifies-brain-areas-altered-during-hypnotic-trances.html.
2. Spence, C., Michel, C., Smith, B. (February 20 2014). "Airplane noise and the taste of umami." *Flavour Journal*, 3. Accessed on Biomedical Central: https://flavourjournal.biomedcentral.com/articles/10.1186/2044-7248-3-2.
3. National Hypnotherapy Society. *Playing with the Senses Can Change How Food Tastes.* National Hypnotherapy Society. Retrieved from https://nationalhypnotherapysociety.org/blog/posts/playing-with-the-senses-can-change-how-food-tastes

7. Ethan's Discovery: Charting a Path to Success

1. Silva, J., & Miele, P. *The Silva Mind Control Method.* Pocket Books, 1989.

8. Glimpse Behind the Veil: Interview with a Visible Subconscious

1. "10 Rules of the Subconscious Mind and How to Harness Them for Your Benefit." *Energy Gardener*, January 12, 2021, https://www.energygardener.com/blog/ten_rules_of_subconscious_mind. Accessed January 13, 2024

10. Seeing The Voice of Reason

1. Dispenza, Joe. *You Are the Placebo: Making Your Mind Matter*. Hay House Inc., 2014. eBook

11. A Visible Subconscious Becomes Her

1. Nova PBS, "Your Brain: Who's in Control?" YouTube, May 31, 2023, video, https://www.youtube.com/watch?v=yQ6VOOd73MA.

14. Real-Life Applications: Tackling Challenges with the Visible Subconscious

1. Tomell, Renee (April 19, 2009). "Subconscious relief: Hypnosis gains acceptance as medical treatment." *The State Journal-Register*. Accessed on August 31, 2023, from https://www.sj-r.com/story/news/2009/04/19/subconscious-relief-hypnosis-gains-acceptance/48741917007/

Conclusion

1. Eagleman, David. *Incognito: The Secret Lives of the Brain*. Vintage, 2011. eBook.
2. Heinrich Popow, "Your mindset determines your tomorrow," *TEDx Talk*, July 5, 2018, video, 18:23, https://www.youtube.com/watch?v=jKICDynQR9g.

ABOUT THE AUTHOR

From a young age, Ponz Manantan, CHt, NLPP, has been captivated by the fascinating aspects of psychology and the logic of computers. His time in Australia sparked his deep exploration into clinical hypnosis and Neuro-Linguistic Programming (NLP).

Born and raised in the Philippines, Ponz moved to Australia before eventually settling in the United States. His insatiable curiosity has driven him throughout his life. With a degree in Computer Science and certificates in Digital Forensics and Clinical Hypnotherapy, Ponz's expertise is a unique fusion of technology and applied psychology.

Ponz enjoys photography, gardening, and ten-pin bowling. His passion for travel goes beyond wanderlust, giving him valuable insights into diverse human behaviors and cultures around the world. Having practiced clinical hypnosis in Washington State, Ponz is interested in pioneering research to enhance mental and physical well-being through innovative concepts.

Made in United States
Troutdale, OR
10/21/2024

24034775R00162